ALSO BY ARLENE FRANCIS
That Certain Something

ALSO BY FLORENCE ROME
The Scarlett Letters
The Tattooed Men

ARLENE FRANCIS

a memoir by

Arlene Francis

WITH Florence Rome

SIMON AND SCHUSTER / NEW YORK

Copyright © 1978 by Arlene Francis and Florence Rome
All rights reserved
including the right of reproduction
in whole or in part in any form
Published by Simon and Schuster
A Division of Gulf & Western Corporation
Simon & Schuster Building
Rockefeller Center
1230 Avenue of the Americas
New York, New York 10020
Designed by Edith Fowler
Manufactured in the United States of America

1   2   3   4   5   6   7   8   9   10

Library of Congress Cataloging in Publication Data

Francis, Arlene.
    Arlene Francis : an autobiography.

    1.   Francis, Arlene.   2.   Actors—United States—
Biography.   I.   Rome, Florence, joint author.
PN2287.F67A32   791'.092'4[B]   77-13701
ISBN 0-671-22808-0

For the men in my life,
Peter and Martin

1

As I climbed into the taxi which drew up in front of radio station WOR, where I do a daily interview show, the driver said, "Hi, Arlene. How's it going?"

Stealing a quick look at his identification card, I replied, "So far so good, Dominick."

"Attagirl, hang in there" was his reply, and I thought to myself, that's exactly what I intend to do, just so long as there are enough Dominicks out there who feel they know me well enough to call me by my first name.

It's true a lot of people in the entertainment world can't stand being accosted by strangers in pursuit of autographs, and if you are a superstar (which, I hasten to add, I am not!), the constant bombardment must be rough. So much so that you may sometimes forget that those very strangers are the ones who helped you make it in the first place.

I know it's disconcerting, to say the least, to be slapped on the back by an admirer when you are dining at a restaurant and about to swallow a mouthful of hot soup, and I will admit to an occasional twinge of annoyance when that has happened. But I quickly remind myself that if you are in the performing arts, even a scalded tongue is preferable to anonymity. If you choose a career that demands that you exhibit yourself, that is part of the price you pay for recognition, and I think that with the possible exception of those with extremely belligerent egos, or some shy reluctant flowers whose only drive for exposure is behind footlights, the rest of us find the words "I thought you were wonderful . . ." second only to "I love. . . ." The critics may have rejected you, but somebody cares. And when the day arrives that nobody cares anymore, that's the time to hang up your eyelashes and retire from the arena.

My own streak or exhibitionism was apparent very early on, and it got me packed off to a convent. I was ten years old, and my father caught me red-handed, playing a ukulele in the window of our apartment in Washington Heights, which is in upper Manhattan. That may not sound like a serious offense. A little flashy, perhaps, calling for a rebuke along the lines of *Whatever-will-the-neighbors-think?* To my father, however, the implications were a good bit more serious. He had a dark suspicion (absolutely correct, as it turned out) that his only daughter had an unseemly, wild desire to, heaven forfend, go on the stage.

To my father, wanting to go on the stage was perhaps a trifle better than, but more or less in the same class with, wanting to work in a house of ill repute, and yes, I *do* know that's an archaic phrase, but it's the only kind of language that seems suited to my adorable, archaic father, Aram Kazanjian.

As Daddy saw it, the three things responsible for having started me down this primrose path were New York City, public school, and my growing awareness of boys. The obvious solution was to remove me from all three.

My mother, however, did not feel that the theater was just another name for a den of iniquity, for her whole cultural background was very different from my father's. However, she was old-fashioned enough not to question her husband's position as Head of the House, and when she was called into conference on *What's-to-be-done-about-Arlene?* she agreed without argument that I was to go to Mount St. Vincent Academy, a proper school for girls, where the nuns would presumably brainwash me of all desire to play the ukulele in the window.

Considering Daddy's rather stern, established sense of behavior, it wasn't easy for him to accept the fact that his father-in-law, my grandfather, Albert Davis, had been an actor. Perhaps that accounted for my mother's more generous view of the theater. Grandfather, as a young man, had toured the provinces of England with a Shakespearean troupe, and he would hold me spellbound with stories of those enchanted hours. It wasn't until years later that I learned he had played the one-line parts that went "Milord, a messenger craves audience," and that he was usually listed in the cast of characters as "A retainer," "A courtier," "Another soldier," and so on. Not that it would have made any difference to me. It was quite enough that he had been (gasp) on the *stage*.

I'm sure Grandfather was the main contributing reason for the way Daddy felt about theater people, because he was hardly the person you'd point to as setting a fine moral example! Naturally I didn't know that. He was plainly and simply marvelous as far as I was concerned, a jaunty, handsome man, with a white beard parted down the middle and a dashing, curling white moustache. With his pink and white English skin and bright, twinkling blue eyes, he looked rather like a rakish Santa Claus—that is, if Santa went around in a high silk hat, wore pince-nez on a black grosgrain ribbon, and carried a malacca cane, all of which were Grandfather's invariable props.

How I admired his grandiose manner, the large theatrical gestures which made everything he said sound so important, and how proud I was to be with him when he would tip a newsboy five whole dollars! (That is, when he *had* five dollars, which wasn't often.) And though it wasn't even whispered in my hearing, Grandfather also did a bit of drinking, so all in all he was the exact antithesis of his strait-laced Armenian son-in-law.

The exhibitionist tendencies in me were fostered and nurtured by Grandfather, who would listen to me recite a poem with as much grave attention as he would have given to Eleonora Duse, only of course he thought I was much more adorable! About that poem—instead of learning Kipling's sturdy warhorse, "Boots," which was a very popular choice with children for boring their parents' friends, I had shrewdly committed to memory a poem by Ella Wheeler Wilcox called "The Two Glasses." It was calculated to reduce Grandfather to an emotional wreck, due to his familiarity with *one* of the glasses.

He would sit down, rest his hands on the cane in front of him, fix me with his eyes and say, "All right, Arlene, center stage." I would curtsy and begin:

> *There sat two glasses*
> *Filled to the brim,*
> *On a rich man's table,*
> *Rim to rim.*

9

Grandfather would nod and his head would come forward slightly, as I continued in a voice as deep as I could make it:

One was as ruddy and red as blood,

And now my voice would change to a trilling soprano:

The other as clear as a crystal flood!

Grandfather's head would start to drop until his chin rested on his hands, and his eyes would begin to fill with tears as I continued the battle between wine and water, water triumphant naturally. I cannot remember all the words, since this was during the Punic Wars when I was about seven years old, but I clearly remember my sense of triumph at being able to move Grandfather to tears. That's when I was hooked. Today Grandfather, Tomorrow the World.

There were other things about Grandfather which must have made Daddy pretty nervous about the theater as a way of life. Grandfather's eye for the ladies, for instance. It was common knowledge that he had done quite a bit of "walking out" with women who happened not to be my Grandmother. The reason it wasn't a secret was that he could boast more begats than the Bible, and what made Grandfather different from your run-of-the-mill roué was a habit he had which I'm sure Father looked upon as theater-oriented—that of bringing his offspring home for Grandmother to rear. What *I* find staggering is that she apparently went along with it all. Moreover, she was as gentle and kind to the children from the wrong side of the sheets as she was to her own.

Grandfather's peccadilloes provided me with some of my favorite relatives, an assortment of uncles and an aunt who was one of the most exquisitely beautiful women I've ever seen. If she took after *her* mother, I can understand Grandfather's straying from the straight and narrow. She was all violet eyes and curling raven black hair, statuesque and very like her father in personality, given to stylish mannerisms, openhanded generosity, quick laughter and sudden tears. She was devoted to me and, along with Grandfather, was sure I was born to go on the stage. A singer herself, she tried to coach me as a singer (it never took), and she gave me some surreptitious lessons in acting: how to walk, stand, project and so on.

Both she and Grandfather actually spoke to Daddy about getting me some professional training, but when they were met with hostile silence, they gave up. Although he was too much a gentleman ever to say so, the very people who were trying to persuade him were the two most cogent reasons he had for not wanting me ever to go on the stage.

However, he did admire feminine grace and charm, so my mother had no trouble convincing him that dancing school would endow me with ladylike airs. Not the Lindy-Hop, Charleston school of dance, no indeed. It was all little white gloves and Mary-Jane slippers and three-quarter time, even though some of the boys danced as though it were judo they were learning.

While I was waltzing we lived in Boston, where I had been born and where my father had a photographic studio. (I'm not going to say when. I intend to be as vague as possible about dates, and if absolutely necessary, to lie. I may say that whenever I'm off speaking at some Town Hall or other, there is a question and answer period, and many of the questions are written on little pieces of paper and handed to me at the luncheon which follows the talk. Inevitably the query arises, "Will you tell us how old you are?" to which I immediately reply, "Five feet five and a half inches. Next question?")

It was through his profession that Daddy met my mother. My aunt had heard about this photographer, whom she described as dark, handsome, mysterious, twirling fierce black moustachios, who *painted* birds, bees and butterflies on a lady's shoulder *or* cheek when he photographed her! Giggling with the wickedness of it all, my mother and aunt went over to have their pictures taken, and sure enough, Father painted a butterfly on Mother's shoulder.

A sidelight on Daddy: as a boy of sixteen he had been an art student in Paris, and one night he dreamed that his family's house in Armenia had been burned down to the ground. In the morning he learned the terrifying truth of the Turkish massacres. His father and mother had indeed been killed.

There was no going home in the face of this holocaust, so he and my uncle Varastad fled to America, where my father apprenticed himself to a photographer. (My uncle, who was to become the remarkable pioneer who in great measure was responsible for the stature which has been achieved in reconstructive and plastic surgery, began as a wire worker in a Boston factory.)

As Daddy grew to manhood, he learned to master the camera, but the desire to be an artist never left him. To a degree he satisfied this longing by painting on his photographic subjects rather than on canvas, and when Mother wandered into his studio with my aunt, he must have *really* been inspired. Taking note of her porcelain beauty—the fragile quality of her transparent skin, the wide, blue eyes, the shimmering gold hair—he painted the most delicate butterfly of his career and began his courtship on the spot by asking permission to call on her.

To jump ahead a bit, after Daddy and Mother were married, he gave up painting butterflies and buttercups on ladies' shoulders and went back to canvas, not as a career, but as a hobby. And how he went back! My recollections of childhood are all tied up with trying to find a light switch, so completely covered with his paintings were our walls.

This all resulted in an agonizing experience after I was grown and married and had a child of my own. Mother and Daddy were living at 530 Park Avenue, and the cumulative effort of Daddy's artistic drive had cut down their living space to the extent that if you were careless in opening a closet, you could very well be struck by a winter landscape or a peacock emblazoned on framed black velvet.

This was around the same time that Mother and I used to haunt a place called the Plaza Art Galleries, where auctions were held. It was great fun, even if you didn't buy anything, and we had become friends with the amiable auctioneers who owned the place, the brothers O'Reilly.

Thinking to make room for a coat, Mother approached Daddy with the splendid idea of having Mr. O'Reilly auction off a few of his lesser masterpieces, which occupied all the space in the closet. The suggestion fell on deaf ears. He argued that they wouldn't know what they were worth, that they wouldn't understand the blood, the sweat, the tears that had gone into their creation, etc., etc.

Mother was very persuasive. "You put whatever price *you* think they're worth on the back of each canvas. That way Mr. O'Reilly will have a guide."

What Mr. O'Reilly needed was a tranquilizer, because after agreeing to auction them, he saw the values Daddy had affixed—$750, $575, $600, and onward through ten canvases. How he arrived at those figures we will never know, but I knew I had better go with Mother to hold her hand during the sale.

If you are only there to observe, the Plaza Art Galleries are great fun, as I have said, but it's hard to work up even a giggle if you're sitting there in a sweat because *you* know Daddy is not Rembrandt by a long shot, and soon everybody else is going to know it too. You wait for jolly Mr. O'Reilly to announce the first canvas. Mother holds on to me for dear life as two men lug it on stage, its back to the audience.

Mr. O'Reilly intones that here is one of several paintings by the well-known artist, Aram Kazanjian (Who? WHO?) and we will start the bidding at $200. While he is making that incredible statement, the two men turn the painting to the stunned audience. It is a mountain of snow with some rabbits in flight, and my heart is pounding so loud, I think it could wake the dead. Not at all. The dead just sit there. Mr. O'Reilly coos and cajoles, his most winning self, but to no avail. The audience is not to be euchred into an opening bid of $200, not with all the blarney of Killarney.

"Ah," ahs Mr. O'Reilly, "I see you're a little slow in starting. Very well, we'll begin at $100!" The same stony silence greets this grand concession, and I am so shell-shocked, I cannot bid to save my darling father's face. My throat is constricted, my eyes are filled, and I feel the heat which has brought the flush to my mother's face. Eventually I am able to put my hand up, which in auctionese passes for a bid, and I buy what is already mine.

And so it went with canvas after canvas, each bird on the wing, each dazzling dogwood, was sold for $35 or $45, mostly to me, and even in retrospect it is painful to remember. At the end of the sale, my terrified mother turned to me and said, "I can't go home, I just can't. It is too humiliating for your father." I soothed her as best I could, said I would sweeten the pot with a few hundred dollars, we would tell him it had been a bad day, very few customers, all poorly dressed. . . .

Now hear this: There is no more powerful protection, no greater force for self-preservation than a proud spirit. My fa-

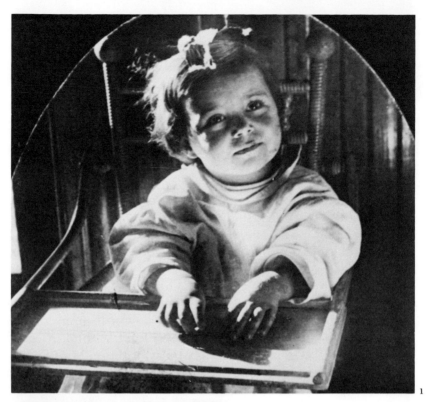

1

2

3

1. As I've always said—"Life is the best potty I've ever attended."
2. Rakish Santa, my grandfather, Albert Davis.
3. "Please hurry, Daddy, my face hurts from smiling!"
4. Daddy and Mother (and baby makes three).
5. April graduate (Mount St. Vincents') with proud mother.

4

5

ther's reaction to the small sale was "What did you expect? What do those people know about art?"

I have described what both my parents looked like, so can there be any question of whom I'd *rather* have taken after? Especially considering all that propaganda about how much more fun blondes have . . . ? It's just lucky for me that I never grew a moustache, because otherwise I'm a ringer for Daddy. Dark eyes, dark hair, olive complexion. (Never mind what you think you see in those pictures. I'm giving you the straight dope.) When I first got my job in television on "What's My Line?" I got my chance to fool Mother Nature whether she liked it or not, because the dark hair created a halo around my face. (I would have liked a halo around my *head,* but this one was bad for the camera.) It was the beginning of restructuring what I had been born with, and since that time I've been twenty different colors and styles, but an English beauty, never!

I think I was about seven years old when Father decided that New York offered greater opportunities for success, and we moved from Boston into that flat on Washington Heights. It was a good move professionally, and when he decided to specialize in children's photographs, he became very successful indeed, one of the best known men in his field.

We lived quite comfortably in what was then a prosperous, middle-class neighborhood, and if I had only been able to curb my passion for ukuleles and picture windows, we might have stayed there. Instead, when they hustled me off to Mount St. Vincent to be saved, my parents moved to the Fieldston-Riverdale section of the Bronx, which at the time was like moving into the country, and we had a big house on a corner up on a hill, surrounded by wide lawns and trees and gardens. It was lovely and open and free, and I thought of it often during those first frightening, miserable days of convent life which were anything *but* free. The temptation to run away would wash over me at times, but the habit of obedience was too deeply ingrained to allow for such rebellion, and I vowed that I would try my best to stick it out.

There are probably some exceptions, but by and large most people in the entertainment world have an inordinate need for approval, for acceptance, for love. I can trace those needs in me back to Mount St. Vincent, and to the fact that I was (at the time that I was there, at least) their only non-Catholic student. Daddy belonged to the Greek Orthodox Church, and my mother to some Protestant sect or other. I had gone to a Presbyterian Sunday school, but only because it was convenient—and I don't think I'd ever even known any Roman Catholics.

I couldn't bear being "different" and I worked day and night at being just like everybody else, only more so. Nobody topped me for diligence when it came to saying prayers, saying my rosary, genuflecting, confessing to sins I hadn't even committed, being, in fact, the most Catholic non-Catholic in the world. My schoolmates, who felt more secure than I, didn't mind bending the rules whenever they could get away with it, but Arlene Francis Kazanjian was obviously bucking for sainthood. There was no way I was going to let a nun humph down her nose and say, "That's what we get for letting a Protestant in the place!"

The only time I ever stepped out of line was to cut some bangs, a coiffure strictly forbidden at Mount St. Vincent, although I still can't figure out what's so sinful about bangs on the forehead. I felt at the time that I had an overriding reason for the infraction of rules, because I had grown a wart on my forehead which one of the ten-year-old doctors in our dormitory told me I could get rid of by tying a hair around it. I did, but it looked so ugly that I cut the bangs to hide it. Whenever the penguins (which is what the nuns looked like to me) were around, I kept the bangs carefully brushed back, but I had forgotten to do that when a nun spotted me in the music room one day. She did it for me, brushing them back none too gently. She also knocked off the wart in the doing, and I was so grateful I almost converted to Catholicism on the spot.

As for ridding me of my yearning for play-acting, the convent not only failed to accomplish that, it did just the opposite. There was a dramatic society of sorts, and there were times when that was the only thing that kept me from reverting to my dream of running away. Poor Father hadn't a clue that the nuns were not only *not* discouraging me, they were actually aiding and abetting me in my degrading ambition!

The graduation play was *The Taming of the Shrew* and, deep-voiced even then, I played Petruchio. My Kate was a hefty classmate swathed in a mile of brocade, and I had to pick her up in my arms and carry her out into the wings as though she were a feather, while she kicked and pummelled me (which she did with a great deal of feeling, I may say). I wasn't even slightly out of breath, and it led the nun who was our dramatic coach to say to my father, "Mr. Kazanjian, I don't think there is any use in your trying to deny to your daughter what she most wants in the world. If she could lift that girl so easily, it shows what she's determined to do with her life." He listened politely and remained unconvinced.

I suppose it says something about me that although I'm certain I *must* have had as much of a little-girl life as anyone, with Hallowe'en and birthday and Christmas parties, with chums named Fluffy and Audrey and Betsy, I can't remember too much about it. Everything I dredge up from my memory has to do with wanting to be an actress.

Well, not quite everything. I *do* remember the awakening of love's sweet young dream, who went by the name of Ashley DeWolfe. Ashley, Ashley, wherever you are, you will never know with what longing I sat on our garden steps at age fifteen, watching for you to come by in your apricot-colored Cunningham (CUNningham!) open convertible, with the apricot-colored poodle sitting alongside you! What were you—seventeen? Eighteen? I suppose about that, because you were fresh out of Horace Mann School for Boys, which was just down the hill from our house. Nor could you possibly have known the contraction of my heart the day you stopped the car, got out, with courtly sophistication said, "My parents have asked me to invite you to have lunch with us at the City Athletic Club on City Island," and handed me a note from them to my parents.

It was pretty heady stuff for me, that first flurry into High Society, and I was terrified that I would commit some dreadful social gaffe which would bring down the scorn of Ashley DeWolfe, his parents, the other polished members of the City Athletic Club, and worst of all, the lordly waiter who handed me the huge menu.

If there is anyone extant who remembers an ad for a language school that pictured a young woman trying to read a menu but unable to because it is in French, consternation written on her face, and the caption that said, "Again she ordered chicken salad," they will know exactly how I felt. I couldn't make head or tail out of what I was looking at, and the only thing which seemed vaguely familiar was called alligator pear salad. *Pears* I knew about, and perhaps alligator pears just meant that they were a special kind of pear, like Macintosh was a special kind of apple, and that they were probably big and green. When my salad arrived, that initial taste was so unexpected that it was all I could do to swallow it, but I did get through lunch without a major disaster, and probably with a reputation as a dainty eater.

As for after lunch, I can only say that to this day, whenever my husband, Martin Gabel, thinks I'm getting a trifle grand, he can always bring me back to earth by raising his eyebrows and saying, "I suppose this is how I must pay for a lovely afternoon." That's because I was stupid enough to tell him I had said that to Ashley DeWolfe when he took me for a stroll in the park, sans parents, and tried to kiss me. Today, any nubile girl over twelve won't believe this, I'm sure, but yes, that's what I said, in what I hoped was a world-weary tone.

To set the record straight, my attitude wasn't all that unique for the times. Properly reared young ladies didn't kiss boys on the first date, and they kept themselves pure for that fellow their parents were always telling them about, a chap named Mr. Right. Mr. R., meanwhile, was somewhere around sullying the kind of girls who listened to sexy talk and did something not even to be mentioned, called "going the limit." At least that's what we were brought up to believe, and I was a good deal too young to understand that public attitudes and private behavior weren't necessarily the same thing. Maybe I was a bit more protected than most girls, because of my strict European father, and because I was an only child. Even a few years later, when I considered myself grown up, I was invited to West Point to a dance and, hold your breath, my *mother* came with me. Poor Lieutenant Linksweiler. It couldn't have been much fun for him to walk a girl and her mother past Kissing Rock.

Mother realized that she couldn't continue the duenna role indefinitely, and eventually I was allowed a little freedom.

I met a lot of boys, got invited to and attended college dances, and you could hardly tell me from any other John Held, jr. girl, hey hey and vo-de-oh-do, as we used to say in the 30s. I corresponded with boys who were away at school, and I contributed to the magazines at the colleges where I had beaux. Bits of poetry by me, signed under the *nom de plume* of "Spark Plug," appeared in the *Lehigh Burr,* the *Cornell Widow,* the *Columbia Jester,* and even in *the* great favorite among college-age people—*College Humor.* Did I say poetry? Judge for yourself: "She told me that she loved me/The color left her cheeks/But on the shoulder of my coat/It stayed for several weeks." Walt Whitman I wasn't.

My dream of being an actress never left me, and when I was graduated from Mount St. Vincent, it almost came to fruition. Our family had many friends who lived in California, so Daddy gave me and Mother a trip out west as a present.

I have to digress for a moment to discuss one of the great scourges of my childhood, my two front teeth, which were widely separated. I hadn't *always* regarded that as a handicap. On the contrary, I could squirt water through that separation farther than anyone on the block. However, as the Good Book says, there is a time for everything. A time to be a water-squirting champion, and a time to look in the mirror and say "Yech!" The latter time had come for me, the terrible realization that I wasn't exactly gorgeous when I opened my mouth (which was quite often).

So off to the dentist to get wired with something called a Jackson adjustable brace. (I'm not sure they make them anymore.) It was called "adjustable" because if the pain became excruciating, you could snap the brace out and rest your roots. The dentist suggested that this not be done too often because the teeth would slide back to square one, and might even endanger my entire upper apparatus. I mastered the agony pretty well, because it was a matter of priorities. How I looked became more important than how I felt. It wasn't *only* vanity. I knew that looks were a working tool if you wanted to be an actress.

End of digression. Mother and I went to California (with my Jackson on my teeth) and to a friend of Mother who knew David O. Selznick. Not only knew him, but knew him well enough to arrange an appointment for me to see him. I suppose it was a little sneaky of Mother, considering how Daddy felt about acting, but as I've said, she didn't feel the same way, and besides, she probably felt nothing would come of it and I'd have had a little excitement.

Up to the very door of his office, I wore my Jackson adjustable brace, and just before knocking at the door, I snapped it out, admired my closely knit uppers in a hand mirror, and went in. A disinterested secretary told me to have a seat, neglecting to tell me I might have it for some time. What did I know about big important producers? I thought you arrived on time, gave your name, and were ushered into The Presence.

Not at all. You sit. And wait. Ten minutes. Twenty minutes. I am in a state of panic. My teeth have started making the return trip. I can feel them move back to where they long to be, and in a frantic state of agitation and with my upper lip immobile, I approach the receptionist and say, "I don't think you understand how urgent it is that I see Mr. Selznick."

She must have seen the agony in my eyes and heard the hysteria in my voice, and maybe she thought he was the father of my unborn child or something, but she did indeed go right in and come out a moment later saying "You may go in now."

"So you want to be an actress," he said, and I, keeping a stiff upper lip so that he wouldn't see the disaster of my teeth, allowed that I did. He told me to walk this way, then that way, turn around, sit down, move my head, and when I was finished he said, "Maybe we can find something for you, but you may have to have something done to your nose." I had the brace in the wrong place all the time!

I did get something in a movie called *Murders in the Rue Morgue*. I was asked if I could swim, and I said yes I could, because the part called for me to float down the Seine, having been dropped through a trap door. Do you know some people can't float? I was one of them, and I went to a friend's house and practised floating in her pool until I was blue and waterlogged, only to have that bit cut out of the picture. No matter, I got some billing:

A Prostitute—Arlene Kazanjian

They also used me on the poster. I was nailed to a cross, dressed in a nightgown which had been ripped off my shoulder, and it was certainly pretty risqué for its time, but I imagine that now it would seem as salacious as Mary Poppins.

In those days it didn't take months of cutting and orchestrating before a picture was released. Once it was finished, it went in the can and got shipped around the country to be shown. Which meant that while Mother and I were still vacationing in California, the picture opened at Loew's State in New York, and sure enough, the poster featuring A Prostitute, Arlene Kazanjian, was prominently displayed in front of the theater. News got around pretty fast, and in no time my father shot off a wire which said, "I HAVE JUST SEEN YOU ALMOST NUDE IN FRONT OF LOEW'S STATE AND SO HAS EVERYONE ELSE. COME HOME AT ONCE." For the time being, that was the end of my movie career.

That autumn I went to Finch Finishing School (before it became Finch College) and got partially finished. There was no more talk of an acting career, certainly not with Daddy, and Grandfather was no longer alive for me to talk to about my hopes and dreams. He had died the year before, bringing immeasurable sadness to me, but there was one memory of his passing that gave me much consolation. My grandmother had been sitting with him, keeping vigil as he faded away, and he summoned up strength enough to turn to her and say, "Would you mind leaving, my darling? I would like the last sound I hear to be the rustle of a woman's skirt." She left the room, and they were the last words he ever spoke so at least he had his final wish.

When I was through with school, Daddy bought me a gifte shoppe on upper Madison Avenue in the gifte shoppe belt, to which we gave the coy name of D'Arlene Studios. The whole idea was to keep me off the streets until I could find a nice rich feller and get married.

Daddy reasoned that now that I'd acquired all that polish, I'd be able to handle the *haute monde,* which would surely beat a path to the door of my shoppe. (Incidentally, "Studios" found its way into the name because Daddy had put a genuine photographic set-up upstairs from the store part, with a photographer on hand to photograph those of my customers who had been shrewd enough to make appointments in advance of coming to shop. We stressed this service in our brochure, and I have been trying to rack my brain to remember if even *one* customer ever availed herself of it. I can't remember any.)

The people who *did* beat a path to our door, just so that they would have a place to come in out of the cold or heat, as the case may have been, were out-of-work actors I'd been meeting here and there. I cultivated them and encouraged them to hang out at D'Arlene Studios because it gave me the illusion of being part of a show-biz crowd—even an unemployed show-biz crowd was better than nothing! Their part of the bargain was to behave like shills, to pretend to be buyers when genuine prospective customers dropped in. They would pick up the wares from the tables on which they were displayed and say things such as "How much is this, Moddom?" and generally make customer noises. My skill in merchandising left a lot to be desired because I had an unfortunate tendency to present my friends with bits of bric-a-brac and pots and pans which they had admired. I figured it was my contribution to the arts.

Less indigent than most of my friends was a young man who had several jobs as a singer on radio shows. He came into the shop one day all excited and said, "Listen Arlene, there's a girl on a radio show I've worked on who plays all sorts of parts—dogs, cats, goats, princesses, beggars—odd bits that call for a trick voice or an accent of some sort. She plays all the bit parts that aren't leads, and she's leaving the show, so they're auditioning people to replace her. I've seen you do imitations and you're pretty good, and this isn't the stage, so maybe your father wouldn't mind if you did that. It's more *business* than show business, and you could say it's *trade*."

It sounded reasonable, but I didn't want to take any chances by mentioning it to my father at all until I'd auditioned. There would be no point in risking a storm in our house if they weren't interested in me. If they were, I'd think of *something*, I simply *had* to. My hunch was that my friend was right and that Daddy would regard radio as something very respectable. It was chiefly an advertising medium, the shows being incidental, and Daddy was respectful of the business world which the commercials glorified. So I went over to see Mr. Donald Stauffer, who at that time did the casting for an advertising agency named Young & Rubicam.

My theatrical credits up to that point consisted of having played Petruchio in *The Taming of the Shrew* in that very off-

Broadway theater called Mount St. Vincent Academy, and the ravaged victim of a madman in *Murders in the Rue Morgue,* but when Mr. Stauffer asked me if I could imitate a cat or a dog, I said of *course,* and woofed and meowed on the spot. I'd have been equally obliging if he'd asked me to try an elephant trumpeting through the forest in search of a mate. Perhaps it wasn't playing Juliet to Barrymore's Romeo, but I was determined to get that job, and I did.

The show was called "King Arthur's Round Table," and even to Daddy that didn't sound like hard-core pornography. Besides, he was really impressed with the salary, which, as I remember, was close to a hundred dollars a week. Not enough to cover us all in rubies, but a sight better than the weekly losses we were sustaining at D'Arlene Studios.

Now it may very well be that hardly a man is now alive who remembers "King Arthur's Round Table," and it is also true that I have felt glowing excitement and pleasure at various times in my career since then, but I have to say that nothing—no kudos, no honors, *no nothing* will ever match the thrill, the absolute delirium I felt on my first appearance on that show. I knew way down in my gut that silly and unimportant as this show might be, it was the beginning of the only career in the world which had any interest for me.

I remember every tiny detail about that evening, the layout of the studio, the sound-effects man, the people in the control room, the actors grouped around the microphones, everybody being especially nice to me because they knew it was my first time around and that I was scared.

Just before a radio program goes on the air, the producer in the control room signals the actors that they are thirty seconds from air time, and that they are to be absolutely quiet, and then he begins the countdown. When that moment arrived on "King Arthur's Round Table," I was so still I had no pulse! To conquer my fright, I closed my eyes and breathed deeply, and a wonderful thing happened. Without summoning it up consciously, a picture of my grandfather, his head resting on his malacca cane, giving me his undivided attention, flashed through my mind. Silently I started reciting:

There sat two glasses
Filled to the brim

On a rich man's table,
Rim to rim . . ."

I saw Grandfather's eyes fill with tears, and suddenly I felt serenely sure of myself. I opened my eyes, saw the studio light starting to flash and knew that we were ON THE AIR.

It didn't scare me in the least. I was ready for the world, thank you very much, Grandfather.

2

No matter what Grandfather thought, I wasn't Eleonora Duse, and no matter what my mother thought, I was no candidate for Miss Universe. Mind you, I wasn't *bad*: I had the required number of eyes, a decent nose despite David Selznick's disparaging comment, and a rather creditable set of teeth, thanks to Jackson's adjustable brace. The wonderful thing was, however, that I didn't *have* to be a pretty-pretty starlet, because in radio it didn't matter what you looked like.

To illustrate: years later—in 1946—I was playing a sexy girl detective, sort of a private eyelash, whose gimmick was that she trapped her quarry with guile and feminine wiles. The show was called "The Adventures of Anne Scotland," and it was broadcast from California, where I was then living. I was married to Martin and *very* pregnant (in that order of course), and *I* could have been called Scotland Yard, because that's how wide I was. I could hardly get close enough to the microphone to speak into it, but my voice still dripped with the breathy nuance of the "C'm up and see me some time" variety.

At one point my friend Claire Trevor, listening to the show in New York, sent me a wire saying, "You don't sound the least bit pregnant but you sound as though you might be at any moment!"

At the beginning of my career, one of the things I had going for me which a lot of girls with the same or perhaps even superior equipment might not have had in such copious quantity, was sheer, dumb luck. Which is not to say that I didn't work exceedingly hard at my various jobs once I got them. It was *getting* them that I'm talking about, the lucky star which seemed to guide me to the right place at the right time, at the precise moment that they happened to be in the market for an ambitious girl who stood 5′5½″ tall, had brown hair and brown eyes and knew how to make animal noises and other compelling sounds. Or else I knew somebody who knew somebody who had some inside information which turned out to be absolutely correct, etc., etc.

I was brought up on Horatio Alger stories, about how you achieve success by keeping your nose to the grindstone, your eye glued to the printed page, your ear to the ground (and your hand in the till, as a cynical friend of mine remarked), but there's hardly a word in any of those books about the roll of the dice. It does seem to be that I had more than my share of good throws, and in case it sounds as though I'm digging my toe in the sand and saying, "Aw shucks," I honestly don't have any false modesty. Even with the best of luck, and no matter who you know, *getting* a job is only a first step. One has to be able to hang on to it, and that, with only one exception, I was always able to do.

The exception was a role I had on that very popular show, "The Goldbergs." Either Gertrude Berg (the author of the series, who also played the leading character) didn't like me, or it could be that I wasn't very good in the part, a possibility which I prefer not to consider! At any rate I was fired, and since that was the first time such a thing had ever happened to me, I was absolutely shattered. It wasn't just the job. It was like having a streak of luck end for you.

Years later I had the sweetest kind of revenge. Mrs. Berg was doing another show out in California, and the studio sent frantic bulletins imploring me to come out. By this time I was doing really fantastically well, and could more or less command my own salary. I commanded one which even I thought was absurdly astronomical, and which I was certain they would turn down. They paid it without a whimper, and I'm sure it's very mean-spirited of me to have gotten such pleasure from that incident, but I sure did. And still do.

The last of my father's objections to my acting career went down the drain because of the nature of radio as a medium. It was clearly designed for family listening at a time when the sex and language revolutions had not even been dreamed of. Considering what one hears and sees now in all media, I would imagine that it is hard (for young people especially) to believe that we could be cut off the air for an unwitting "hell" or "damn," or for anything which could even remotely be interpreted as an aspersion on an ethnic or racial group. Maybe it's apocryphal but I heard that a network cut "that's like the pot calling the kettle black" for fear of its being interpreted as a racial slur. It *could* have happened. (While I'm about it, I have to say that although it is true that we carried things to extremes of silliness on occasion, I'm by no means convinced that what goes on now is all that much of an improvement. Even though I am violently opposed to censorship, I wish there were some canons which would guide broadcasters on their own, such as that nice old-fashioned word, "taste.")

It was not a position of highly moral attitudes which accounted for such sensitivity on certain subjects, by the way. Sponsors were touchy about them for the very practical reason that they might offend potential customers. After all, people who lived in what is called "the Bible belt," or who belonged to this or that religious or racial group, ate as much cereal and used as much soap as anyone else! Nevertheless, in spite of all the no-nos and the must-dos, a lot of good, amusing, serious and informative programs were broadcast every day, and like Topsy, the industry growed. And I growed with it.

There was hardly a major show I didn't get to play in at one point or another. "The March of Time," "Cavalcade," and soap opera after soap opera—twenty or more. So many that I'd run from one studio to another in the same day, changing my accent en route: from "Big Sister" to "Aunt Jenny," from "Stella Dallas" to "Mr. District Attorney" (from Natchez to Mobile, yeahhhh). I'd pick up the script they handed me at the door, run through it with the other members of the cast and *bam*, we were on the air. That, incidentally, was a trick which radio people had mastered and which theater people were usually not quite so expert at—the ability to read through a role in one rehearsal and be practically character perfect the first time. Theater people had no use for such gimmickry, for they had time; time to rehearse, to study, to absorb a role so that they fully and deeply understood what they were doing

26

and saying. We, on the other hand, were slaves to a stopwatch. Every second of air time cost thousands of dollars, and as we were "live" (nothing was taped in those days—there was no such thing, I believe), we were all acutely aware that mistakes, fumbles of words and sentences, were fatal, for time literally was money.

That didn't mean that we didn't all do our level best to give the characters we were playing a feeling of reality, but anything resembling depth of characterization which filtered over the air waves was purely accidental, as a rule. What passed for rehearsal was usually the director timing the script to see if we needed any cuts, or perhaps correcting a pronunciation here and there. Once we were on the air, the director in the control room told us to go faster or slower, indicating the former by sending his finger around in a circle, and the latter by stretching his hands apart. If everything was fine, he placed his finger on his nose. That was the semaphore for the radio industry.

If we didn't learn much about acting, we certainly learned a lot about discipline and timing—invaluable assets in any medium, and an absolute necessity in radio. And we had fun. Tremendous fun. The kind of fun that comes when you're all in something together, something that is still fairly new, bursting with success, flexing its muscles all over the place, and you are part of it! It gave us all a sense of community, of camaraderie.

Daddy liked the idea that I was in a business where people spoke so well of things like Rinso, Spry, Anacin, Ipana, Wheaties and such, for surely shows which were sponsored by General Mills, General Foods, General Motors and General Electric (my father was respectful of generals) would not be cast in offices where there were casting couches. No hankypanky there. No sir. Not like those Broadway fellows. I could never bring myself to tell him that the men in grey flannel suits over on Madison Avenue could make it around a desk just as fast as their Broadway counterparts.

As for my mother, she was positively ecstatic at the way things had worked out. For her, it was the best of all possible worlds, for despite the fact that she had been my secret ally in my desire to be an actress, she was a lady down to her fingertips, a lady in the old-fashioned sense. *Her* idea of a great actress was Billie Burke, and she had secretly trembled at the thought that I might become involved in something which she would consider coarse or vulgar. Radio allowed her to put aside her fears.

Another thing. From my point of view I was getting to be a bloody plutocrat, running from soap to soap. It wasn't that they paid me so much (I think it was around twenty-five dollars per episode), but five episodes a week on two or three different daytime shows, then a higher salary on an evening program, and it added up to enough to make it advisable that we close up ye olde gifte shoppe, which my mother had tried to keep going while I pursued my new career. I was now officially an actress. (Officially means you pay your union dues.)

What I didn't mention to my parents was that I would have given up "Pepper Young" and his whole family for a decent role in a good show on Broadway. Or even in a show that wasn't all that good. They would have considered me a certifiable lunatic if they had known I was willing to jeopardize what I was building in the way of income and fame, for a chance at a role in a show which could close overnight.

To be entirely honest, that fame and income got to be very important to *me* too, without my even realizing it. I was offered a number of Broadway shows after a bit, and I did them, too—provided that they didn't interfere with my radio or TV schedules. I didn't stop to analyze it at the time, but it does occur to me now that someone who is a dedicated theater person doesn't set up roadblocks such as "if I can fit it in conveniently."

There is no question, however, that I was split right up the middle on that subject, and I thought of it a few years back when I was going through some old papers and ran across a telegram from an agent. I had saved it because I couldn't bear to part with it, and it read: "I HAVE AN OFFER FOR YOU TO DO VIRGINIA WOOLF FOR FIVE THOUSAND DOLLARS A WEEK FOR SIX WEEKS." I was so flattered at the time I received it that I could hardly speak. My mother had been visiting me, and I showed it to her without comment.

After reading it, she handed it back to me as though it were contaminated and said, "Arlene, please don't ever do a play like that while I am alive." It's hard to believe that even at that point, when I was a married woman with a child, I still couldn't consider doing something my mother didn't want me to do, even play a role which under any other circumstances I would have *paid* five thousand dollars a week to get.

I'm not proud of that story, and I tell it only to illustrate what I think is an essential flaw in my character. I find it terribly hard to speak up or behave in a way that will arouse anger against me, and though I've gotten a little better about that now than I was as a young girl, it still raises hell with me when I am forced to take a position which won't win me a popularity contest. Nevertheless, now I *do* do it. On occasion.

I might *never* have been able to had it not been for Martin. Thanks to his coaching, the worm has turned from time to time, and I always feel triumphant when it happens. As a matter of fact, at first Martin could hardly believe my reticence was genuine, but when he finally came around to understanding that it was, he got to work on the problem. He was Professor Higgins and I was Eliza, except that instead of saying, "The rain in Spain stays mainly in the plains," he kept hammering at me, "You must learn to speak out!" I would mumble, "Sure, sure," and then forget it.

But his words seeped into my unconscious and one day they fought their way forward. It was during the time that Senator Joseph McCarthy was behaving like a road company Hitler without even the excuse of believing what he said. I'm not going to rehash that period here, for it has already been documented so much, except to say that the headlines McCarthy sought had often been achieved at the expense of the lives and careers of some of our dear friends. I was hardly in a mood to be charitable or objective about a man whom I considered to be a monster, and it was during this period that we were invited one evening to dine at Lester Markell's house.

Lester Markell was at that time the editor of the Sunday *New York Times* Magazine, and many of his guests that evening were journalists. Among them were Alicia Patterson, the publisher of *Newsday*, and her husband, Captain Harry Guggenheim. ("Captain" was a holdover-title from a commission he'd held in the Navy.) I was a bit shy among these brainy and articulate people, so for the most part I kept my mouth shut.

In the course of dinner, Captain Guggenheim made conversation by describing an incident of the day before. He told us how he had been waiting for his car, which was late in arriving, and Senator McCarthy had driven up and offered him a lift. I was waiting for him to tell us how he had said, "Ride with you, you bastard? I'd rather have cholera," or some such thing, instead of which he described McCarthy as this charming, gracious man, so witty, so adorable, I almost suffered a cardiac arrest. I could bear it for only a little while, and I suddenly heard myself saying, "Captain Guggenheim, if you don't stop talking about Senator McCarthy that way, I'm going to slap you."

I don't remember anything that happened after that, but I do remember Martin's face. His jaw dropped open because he had never, never heard me speak out before. He didn't say, "By George she's got it," but clearly, he was absolutely delighted with me. I also remember that Mrs. Guggenheim came over and sat beside me and tried to soothe me so that nothing else would happen. Little did she know that I'd shot my bolt, but the entire incident still gives me pleasure to recall.

Because it *is* so difficult for me to cope with unpleasantness, I can't even toss aside the crank letters which I get from time to time. Everybody who is exposed to the public gets them, and I *know* that, so wouldn't you think I'd have sense enough just to throw them in the trash basket where they belong? Instead of which I behave as though they had been written by responsible people, rather than by kooks who have nothing to do but vent their hate in vile attacks and obscenities. I'm not talking about reasoned letters which take issue with a position I might take, or which go to the trouble of correcting me when I have been in error about something. It is the other kind that throw me, that really succeed in depressing me. "Why should that person hate me?" I ask myself, and of course there is no answer.

What I've learned from this is that if you put all your energies into being affable and agreeable, it's true you're going to make a lot of friends, and that part is good. BUT, it is very costly in terms of emotional repression, and that part is bad. Somebody should have told me when I was a little girl that the whole world doesn't have to think you're adorable. Instead they told me that I could catch more flies with honey than with vinegar, that if I smiled the whole world would smile with me, and that a soft answer would turneth away wrath. Or in basic English: Don't make waves.

But as long as we're talking in clichés, let me try this one on: You can't have everything. I may never have had the satisfaction of being the greatest Lady Macbeth in the history of the theater, for example, because I didn't have the courage to give up everything else and concentrate on the stage (never mind whether I'd have been able to play her in any case!), but what I did and do have is not to be minimized.

It has been a marvelous, exhilarating life with tremendous rewards, and I'm not speaking only of the financial rewards, although I'm not pretending to ignore them. I mean rewards in terms of personal satisfaction, the kind that come of meeting and sometimes being lucky enough to become friends with many of the most stimulating, exciting people in the world. Radio and television interviews have made it possible for me to have known Helen Keller, Carl Sandburg, Mrs. Roosevelt . . . to meet the Queen of England, the Prince of Wales, and the Duke of Ellington . . . to have a hug from Gregory Peck and a peck on the cheek from Jimmy Carter. And all those things as just part of the day's work. That's not likely to happen to Lady Macbeth!

There was quite a group of us running from studio to studio trying to earn a living in those early days. A lot of people fell by the wayside, but for a surprising number of us with the stamina to stick it out, the parts got bigger and the careers loomed brighter. For instance, I finally got to be the star of an opus called "Betty and Bob," or rather the co-star, because Bob was played by Van Heflin. And scrabbling along in our eager pack of young hopefuls were Garson Kanin, Kirk Douglas, Joseph Cotten, Agnes Moorehead, Faye Emerson, Orson Welles, Mike Wallace, Claire Trevor—and oh yes, have I mentioned Martin Gabel?

Well, it isn't really fair to classify Martin Gabel with me as a young hopeful, because he was playing the *lead* on a soap opera called "Big Sister." (The sponsor was Rinso, and in the course of time the Rinso WHITE commercial was sung by a chubby little girl with a soaring voice named Beverly Sills!) Martin played the husband of Big Sister herself—Alice Frost, who was one of the giants in the medium—and he had *the* most terrific speaking voice on radio, I think, or anywhere else for that matter. Still has. It was Ronald Colmanish, only deeper, with that same fine shading and enviable diction. He is rather fond of pointing out that listeners sent in Rinso box tops and quarters by the million to get his photograph, and I can't deny it because I was there, and it's true. I had only a tiny bit part on that show and I stood in such awe of him that I was afraid to talk to him, and that's true too. Well, almost true.

The real reason I was afraid to talk to him was that I thought he was a bit of a stuffed shirt, because he never joined in the fun and games around the studio with the rest of us. He was Mr. Star, and how! We exchanged greetings sometimes and that was it. But one day I saw him coming into the drugstore-cum-restaurant in the CBS building where we all hung out, and I wanted a favor, so I walked over to him.

I knew that Martin was a skilled Broadway actor in addition to being a radio favorite, and that he was involved with Orson Welles in the Mercury Theater productions, so I said to him, "Mr. Gabel, Mr. Welles is going to do *Danton's Death* and I understand that there is a part in it for a lady of the evening." (It sounded so much more "refaned" than whore, which I didn't think was a very ladylike word to use.)

"Yes?" he said, raising his eyebrows, and I was immediately so intimidated that I stumbled along on how my voice made me more suitable for such parts than for ingenues, and I had played such a role in *Murders in the Rue Morgue,* and did he possibly think he could mention me to Mr. Welles?

"We'll see," he said, "let me think about it."

I don't know what he had to think about, but he *did* mention it to Orson, I *did* audition, and I got the part.

It was not my first role on Broadway. I had hung around casting offices and gotten jobs on my own by now—some walkons, some one-liners, some understudies, minor parts all. I'd worked in summer stock as well, every chance I'd had, and with one thing and another I had accumulated some experience in the theater.

Well, you could *call* it experience. I remember one job in a show called *La Gringa,* with Claudette Colbert, in which I played a neophyte nun, and I stood around with another nun on the stage, both of us playing with our rosaries and mumbling prayers that went "Hail Mary full of grace isn't that Moss Hart in the third row?" or "Our Father which art in Heaven can you let me have five bucks until Friday?" and so on. Miss Colbert went straight to Hollywood from that show, and I'm afraid nothing much happened to me except that I got used to the feel of a stage underfoot and I no longer blinked at the lights. If that constitutes experience . . .

Eventually my father allayed his fears about the theater, and the time arrived when he felt *entirely* safe about me, and that was because I was no longer his responsibility. By the time I asked Martin to intercede on my behalf with Orson Welles, there was somebody else in charge—my husband, Neil Agnew, who had all the qualities my parents had prayed for in a son-in-law; he was rich, reliable, handsome, socially acceptable and devoted to me. He was, in short, the man of *their* dreams, and he took over their function, assuming not just the role of husband, but of loving parent, fond and protective. They couldn't have been happier.

Unfortunately, *I* could have been.

3

I met Neil while I was understudying Claire Trevor in a play called *The Party's Over*. I hadn't much to do during rehearsals except sit in the auditorium and pray that Claire would get a minor ailment that wasn't too serious so that I could go on for her and be discovered.

Now there was this terribly attractive "older" man who was also sitting around the auditorium a good bit of the time, and as I knew he wasn't understudying anyone, I asked around to find out who he was and what he was doing there. It developed that he was an executive of Paramount Pictures, which had an investment in the production, and I could understand that he might feel it important that he look in occasionally in order to guard the investment. However, he spent so much time there that it seemed to me he was guarding it beyond the call of duty. Oftener and oftener he guarded it sitting with me, and I was pretty flattered that this man of the world seemed to find me attractive.

He was courtly and handsome, and not at all like my free-wheeling friends, most of whom were scrambling around as I was, theatrical gypsies who hadn't time (or money) for the sort of things Neil was accustomed to. He squired me around to chic little night clubs where the tab for a bite of supper was as much as most of my dates could earn in a week. My chums were still in the spaghetti, red wine, candlelight and gypsy violin stage, and it was quite a revelation to be courted with flowers, gifts and dazzling attention. I really did think of him as an older man, and though the thought gave me pause, I came to the conclusion that fifteen years was not exactly an insurmountable barrier. He was witty and cozy and I loved being with him.

I got a little nervous when Neil started talking about marriage. I had loved the courtship part, but marriage hadn't occupied my mind because for one thing, he was already married, although separated from his wife. For another thing I had a serious beau about whom he knew nothing, Johnny Green, the talented song writer and musical conductor, who was also madly attractive. As it happened, he *too* was married, he *too* was separated from his wife, but he *did* know about Neil, and he was quite disturbed about it.

Johnny was conducting the dance band at the St. Regis Roof, and he would invite me to come up, and get me a little table all to myself, off to the side. He'd send loving looks in my direction as I waited for him to join me between sets, or to take me to supper when his night's stint was over. It was *toujours-gai* time, very New Yorkerish in the manner of those B movies Hollywood used to grind out back there in the 40s when all this was happening, and I loved every minute of it. You could even write the plot of that movie: aspiring young actress must choose between debonair, aging suitor with great influence in the entertainment industry (played by Adolphe Menjou) and struggling young composer-conductor (played by Cary Grant). Except of course that Neil was not exactly aging, and Johnny was hardly struggling, having already acquired quite an ASCAP rating, thanks to songs like "Body and Soul," among others.

It never got to that point, actually. After a bit, Johnny and I mutually agreed that we weren't meant for each other. We parted quite amiably, and I decided to marry Neil.

Yes, I had misgivings, but they were so terribly vague. There was nothing I could point to as a flaw, nothing about which I could say, "I don't like this" or "I don't like that," but something, I wasn't sure what, seemed to be missing in our relationship. I attributed it to the fact that we lived in different worlds, and that all it would require was getting used to. Nevertheless, doubts sometimes haunted me in the middle of the night, and I'd say, "Perhaps I ought to call it off, give myself a little more time—" and I'd answer myself by saying, "Did anyone ever tell you you're crazy? Here's this marvelous, considerate, divine, handsome man who adores you, and what is there even to think about?"

And so we were married.

I knew I was making a mistake even while the ceremony was in progress. Now I ask you, what do you do if that happens? Tap the judge on the arm and say, "Hold the phone please. I've just had this blinding flash of intuition that tells me it isn't going to work?" Yes, I suppose you can do that. Then you can stand back and wait for the men in the white coats to come and get you, while your parents have fainted dead away and your bridegroom is standing there glassy-eyed with shock. I don't know. Maybe there are some people who could manage it, and I sometimes have wished that I'd done just that. However, my reaction to my misgivings was to pray that I was wrong and to vow to make a success of my marriage. Clearly, the way to do that was to lay aside my qualms and attribute them to garden-variety bride's jitters, a not uncommon phenomenon as everybody knows.

A small aside: My wedding night was spent in the now defunct Hotel Ambassador, which was on Park Avenue. Given the mores of the 40s, particularly as they applied to us convent-bred girls, I had no foreknowledge of my groom's sleeping habits. The fact, for example, that he had a most inharmonious snore! I watched in hypnotic wonder to see how long it would take for the breath he drew in to be released. At times it was touch and go. Clearly there was no sleep for me under those circumstances, so would you believe that I spent my bridal night bundled up in the bathtub with the water running full blast in the sink to drown out the competition?

For those who like to tug at their beards and go in for weighty Freudian interpretations, I submit the following. A few weeks after we were married, we went to the Laurentian Mountains for a little vacation, which we hadn't been able to take right after the wedding owing to our separate work schedules.

We stayed at a lodge, a beautiful place, surrounded by magnificent forests. There were golf courses and riding trails, and these things were perfect for both of us because Neil loved golf and I loved riding. I was a fair rider, nothing Billy Steinkraus would have tapped for the Olympics, but not bad.

36

One day, while Neil was off playing golf, I went riding with a group along one of the trails, and as we came out of the woods, the horse I was on realized that he was on his way back to the stable and he broke into a gallop. I wasn't prepared for it and I was thrown, momentarily knocked out.

I had fallen on my coccyx and it hurt like the devil, but I didn't seem to have broken anything, so as soon as I could make it, the other members of our party helped me back on the horse. That's the time-honored theory: after a fall, if you get back on the horse you'll never be afraid to ride. All well and good, but *I* wasn't afraid because *I had no idea of what had happened.* Except for the pain in my rear, I didn't remember falling, I didn't remember getting back on. Literally. I rode back to the stable in a complete fog, not sure of anything, including whether I ought to ask these amiable strangers with whom I was riding and who seemed so concerned about me, exactly where we were and exactly who I was. I decided that on the whole, it would be better if I just kept my mouth shut and listened for clues.

As I didn't know my name, it worried me that I wouldn't know what key to ask the hotel clerk for when I got to the desk, but he took care of that problem for me by saying, "Here's your key, Mrs. Agnew. I heard about your fall. Are you sure you're okay? Is there anything we can do?"

I assured him I was *fine,* simply fine, and privately I was certainly relieved to learn that I was Mrs. Agnew, and that I had a room in which to lie down.

I don't know if I can describe how agonizing it is not to know who you are. I lay on my bed for hours in a torment of thoughts. Who was *Mr.* Agnew? What had my maiden name been? How long had I been married? I looked around the room for pictures or clues and as luck would have it there was just nothing around. Or if there was, I was too bewildered and rattled to know where to look.

When Neil came into the room looking terribly concerned, I assumed he must be Mr. Agnew, and my eyes filled with tears. He came right over and put his arms around me, and I blurted it all out, about the accident, about how I felt. He already knew about the accident—he had been told about it at the desk—and on the subject of my amnesia, he was as gentle, as dear as though he were talking to a child. He ex-

6

7

8

6. H.R.H. Arlene Kazanjian—
pictured at home.
7. Proprietress "D'Arlene Studios"
(dressed for work).
8. We Armenians are always down
to earth.
9. The young Mrs. Neil Agnew
(with the young Otto Von B.) at
the farm in Southbury, Conn.
10. As a brand-new bride—astride
Prince, clutching a terrified Otto
Von Bismarck.

9

10

plained that he was my husband, that he had been playing golf, and that when they had told him I had been injured he had immediately sent for a doctor, who was now on his way over. Above all, I was not to worry about what was happening in my head. I would be better soon and everything would come back to me.

The amnesia lasted twenty-four hours, twenty-four *terrifying* hours, and I can well imagine the anguish which others who have not had such quick recoveries must suffer. Not to know who you are, to have everything erased, wiped out entirely—it is truly horrendous. But to get back to that amateur psychoanalytic interpretation, it could certainly be argued that being Mrs. Neil Agnew was something I wished very much not to be, and *that* reality was something I was trying to erase from my mind. (All very good, but who told the horse to throw me?)

In view of the fact that Neil was the most gracious, considerate husband one could have, it seems coldly ungrateful of me to have been so unloving. He was wonderful to my family, far beyond the ordinary son-in-law's responsibility. He needed no prompting from me to ask them to dinner, or to invite them to come with us to the house we had in Southbury, Connecticut. As a matter of fact, he gave my father several acres of land on our property so that my parents could build a house next to ours. I don't think it was a deliberate plan to bind me close to him. I feel sure he didn't think he had *need* of such plans. No, he was genuinely fond of them, and they of course loved him.

All of which made it terribly difficult for me when, a few short years later, I finally reached the point where I had to end my marriage or lose my sanity. And all through those years, I never hinted by word or look that I was anything but happy. It was as though I lived at two different levels, one so deeply buried that most people, particularly the principals in the case, were not even aware that anything was amiss. The other, the smiling young matron was so real that even I didn't always recognize her for what she was—a facade. We sometimes begin to believe the personalities we assume, in order to protect ourselves. Nobody likes to look in the mirror and say, "You're a fake!"

If I've led anyone to think that my marriage to Neil was

one long torment of crying into my pillow, it was nothing of the sort. We had some wonderful times together, and though I wasn't in love with him, he was certainly lovable, and I *was* tremendously fond of him—which in some ways made things even harder for me. It was a bit like a father-daughter relationship, but I already had a devoted father and as in many things, one was enough.

Most of Neil's friends were more of my parents' generation than of mine, which amplified the illusion in my mind that I was the bright youngster, being charming to her parents' coterie. They were the people who had already arrived, their goals had been accomplished, whereas most of my companions were either just starting up the road or warming up in the bullpen. I respected, though with a speck of fearsome awe, the motion picture executives who peopled his world—but I could hardly put them on the same plane as my buddies with whom I swapped information in Walgreen's Drug store about who was casting for what.

The truth is that Neil was infinitely better than I at generation-gap bridging. He treated my friends with boundless courtesy, had a great gift for making them feel warmly welcome at any time, conveyed with thoughtful gestures his affection for them, and with no urging on my part, he would invite them up to our farm. He really did enjoy their company, but chiefly he wanted me to be happy.

The people with whom he was accustomed to spending time were his business associates, and as I have said, they were the strong men of the industry. One was Spyros Skouras, who ran Paramount's Sales Department. He was a Greek who bore his gifts with great goodwill and generosity. He and his gentle wife were the first guests in our newly decorated home, and I was your standard shaky bride whose husband's boss was coming to dinner.

We lived on Park Avenue (where else?) in one of those wonderful old buildings with great high ceilings and fireplaces, and while the entire apartment was *House Beautiful* material, the dining room was positively a decorator's delight. Since it had more entrances than a French farce, it had been decided by my decorator that the room lacked "serenity," and a circular trolley was devised inside the square of the ceiling, from which was dropped a cascade of grey velvet to the floor.

Closed, it covered the back door, the hall, the kitchen door and the entrance to the bar. By pulling a cord these openings could be revealed one at a time with the same splendid drape as the Metropolitan Opera curtain!

So now for the evening's entertainment. Behold the grey velvet drape up on the bar side, and the graceful hostess with the hors d'oeuvres tray, as her handsome husband prepares drinks for Mr. and Mrs. Skouras. Enter from the back-door drape Frieda, the young German cook with a comedy accent second only to Jack Pearl's Baron Münchausen, except that hers is genuine. Accompanying Frieda, and a match for her in lineage if not in shape, is our German dachshund, Otto Von Bismarck (and what would *you* name a dachshund if you were young and oh so clever?). Enter is not actually the right word. *Bursting in* is more like it, and Frieda, obviously totally unawed by the surroundings or guests, announces, "Mrs. Ach-new, Otto hass vorms!"

I am aghast. I pretend she hasn't said what she has said. I hiss, "Thank you, Frieda," hoping she will think that's an end to it, and I trill out, "Mrs. Skouras, can I interest you in some quiche?"

Frieda is undaunted. She continues, "Otto hass vorms unt I know it becuss he vass sliding on his backsite in der eleway-ter." Quite an icebreaker that, but I wanted to die of embarrassment, and I wanted to kill Frieda, just before I killed myself. It's awful to feel you've goofed first time around.

On the other hand, when I wasn't under the pressure I'd felt on that particular occasion, Frieda gave me many a good giggle. I overheard her ordering our groceries over the phone one day. "Listen, Mrs. Ach-new likes pwoons but not der lid-dle vons, you should send me some pwoons as bik as an ekk." During the silence following that statement she pursed up her lips and, when it was her turn to speak again, she burst out, "Lissen, your ekks aren't so bik eidder!" and slammed down the receiver. Yes, I was crazy about Frieda. When she met me at the door with "Velcome Mrs. Ach-new, I yust changed der vater on der pussy villeys," my world seemed all right. I was hoarding giggles just about then.

Neil and I were married for five years, and I think one of the reasons it lasted *that* long was my absorption in work, and the fact that Neil understood that facet of my character and was enormously supportive at all times . . . even though it was quite possible that he would have preferred that I stay at home and join the ranks of executive wives who made careers of being just that. In his milieu, such wives were tremendously important assets (if they did their jobs well) in helping to further their husband's careers. It is a rather elaborate and involved game, the one that is played along the wife-circuit, where entertainment and gossip and undercover information are all part of the game-plan, and I am afraid that even if I hadn't been a working woman myself, I would have been poorly equipped to take part in it.

If Neil had wanted that from me, he never indicated it in any way. He understood perfectly how important it was to me to have my own career, and he never denigrated it in any way or asked me to put it in abeyance, even when there were conflicts in our schedules.

There *were* such times, occasions when I knew that he would have liked to have me go with him to one place or another—California, Chicago, Detroit, wherever there happened to be a sales meeting, when it would have been nice to have a wife along. Once, out walking, he told me the Paramount offices might all be moved to the West Coast. I panicked at the thought of leaving New York just as my career was getting under way. I must have wailed, "Oh Neil." He said ruefully, "How far west would you go for me, Sixth Avenue?"

He never again said a negative word when I apologized for not being able to come because I had to work, and his only objection was that he felt I was working too hard for the sake of my career and ignoring my physical limitations. How do you ask a man like that for a divorce? *I* found it impossible, even though I knew after I'd been married for two years that there was no possibility I could make the marriage work.

In the course of those years, I tried to bring myself to the point of saying so about a thousand times, but I never made it. I told myself that my reason for being so cowardly was that I didn't want to cause him any pain, or to make my parents unhappy. Well, I never claimed to be brave.

4

Martin Gabel's intercession with Orson Welles on my behalf introduced me to the most vital and exciting theater I had ever experienced up to that point. The part I got wasn't terribly big or important, but I treasured my notices, which contained such ecstatic words as "competent"and "all right." The first was from Burns Mantle, the second was from Walter Winchell, but considering that Winchell had hated every minute of the play, words like "all right" seemed like an accolade! The important thing to me was that I had been noticed at all.

Despite Winchell, it was a terrific show. A bit intellectual for *his* taste, because he had sort of a reverse snobbery, which took the form of putting down anything he considered to be "arty," which is to say anything with words of more than one syllable, but *chacun,* as they say, to his *mauvais goût,* as long as we're being arty.

To me, there were so many things about *Danton's Death* which were memorable, not the least of which was Orson Welles himself. I thought then and I think now that Orson was genuinely touched with genius. His concepts were brilliant, daring, not wedded to custom and, in large measure, his detractors were people who were nervous about things which were off the beaten track. New concepts sometimes threaten people who are accustomed to doing things in a certain way, and mavericks seem to arouse their ire. But to all of us who worked with him, Orson was an inspiration, end of commercial.

Among his innovations for *Danton's Death* was a scenic idea. A hole was cut in the center of the stage, so that that part of the stage could be lowered to change a scene, while the actors on the stage played another scene around the opening. I have a very good reason for remembering this particular aspect of the staging, because Martin and I were in the scene that got dropped into the cellar to be changed, and we stayed there every night for five or ten minutes before we got hauled up again. I think that's what movie scenario writers call "meeting cute," and although we *had* met, we certainly got to know each other a lot better in that dark, dank cellar.

To look at Marty you wouldn't have dreamed that he had the important attributes of Lothario. He looked rather more like a serious banker, but I just happened to know that he had quite a reputation as a ladies' man, because several of the ladies whose man he was were friends of mine. Alone with him in that cellar, I began to understand why they found him so attractive, because he positively radiated a certain romantic charm. Not that I took him seriously, but that terrific voice whispering sweet talk in my ear generated a lot of excitement. I pretended that those "darling, you're glorious" phrases with which he seduced me were standard actor chit-chat (which, by the way, they could very well have been. Actors are constitutionally incapable of just saying "hello," and they greet each other with extravagant gestures and language which could get them arrested in real life). Thus when Martin would say, "You silly little thing, don't you know I love you?" I would answer in kind and then laugh to show him that I wasn't serious either. Not in the least. Hah. I was married, wasn't I?

I never got to be a shining star of the Mercury Theater, but I learned a great deal about acting, much of it from Martin who was not only a wonderful actor, but a wonderful teacher. And of course I have already said that Orson was an inspired director who, by his own enthusiasms, seemed to free you as an actor to go beyond anything you thought yourself capable of.

I did a number of other shows with the Mercury Theater: *Horse Eats Hat* (in which another little-known actor named Joseph Cotten played the lead, and for which Paul Bowles, then a gifted unknown, wrote the music). We did *Heartbreak House* too, and a modern dress version of *Julius Caesar* which was the talk of the town, and it was all wildly exciting. John Houseman was part of the group, and that was the clue to everything—

there were no stars, just members of the group. They were good, every one of them, so good in fact that when Martin played Cassius in *Caesar,* he was so convincing as the villainous plotter that there was never so much as a titter on the line, "Yon Cassius hath a lean and hungry look." Quite a tribute to his ability, considering that Martin was constantly dieting, without too much success. The only one who seemed to take notice of his girth was reviewer George Jean Nathan who, after praising Martin's performance, wrote, "Martin Gabel played the lean and hungry Cassius looking as though he'd eaten Dinty Moore's out of house and home." Martin hath a much leaner and hungrier look now, but he still diets.

All of this was happening at a time when I was beginning to move ahead in radio. While I still had all the shows I've mentioned, "Betty and Bob," "Mr. District Attorney," "Portia Faces Life"—you name it, I was on it—I got a new program which set the pattern for much of my future career. I became hostess of a game show called "What's My Name?" I shared honors with the host, Budd Hulick, who had achieved a big reputation as a wit when he was the Budd of "Stoopnagle and Budd," a zany show which featured a very special and superior brand of humor.

"What's My Name?" was one of the first game shows on radio, and the contestants were selected from the audience. Budd and I impersonated various figures in public life and gave a series of clues to each contestant. If they guessed who we were supposed to be on the first clue, they got the terrific sum of ten dollars; on the second clue, nine dollars, and so on. The day of the unreal prizes, the sixty-four-thousand-dollar-question days, had not yet arrived. On our show we were so modest it wasn't even worthwhile cheating, but everybody seemed to have just as much fun.

The reason "What's My Name?" was so important in my life was that it was my first experience with ad-libbing, of saying things which came into my head instead of sticking to a written script. Budd was an old hand at that sort of thing, and I had to think very fast to keep up with him. I found that I loved doing it, that in fact I was pretty good at it. Better than I thought I'd be. And naturally, I got so cocky about how good I was that I managed to overdo it now and then, to trip over my own tongue, saying things which I realized in mid-sentence oughtn't to be said on the air.

The periods during which we were supposed to ad-lib were just before the game itself, and again when it was over. The pre-game ad-lib was for the purpose of making the contestants feel a little less nervous—keep their teeth from chattering and their knees from knocking. And after the game, Budd and I would indulge in a spot of banter with them—well, everyone's seen game shows, and they all work more or less alike, even now.

On one occasion we had a contestant who was visiting from Ireland, and when he correctly guessed who I was pretending to be after two questions and I handed him his eight dollars, I said, in what I hoped was an endearing tone with a touch of brogue, "And how many pints of beer would *that* buy you in Ireland?"

Well! You would have thought I'd said "Burn the Vatican!" It was not our contestant who felt that way, but Indignant Listeners, who sent me a passel of Indignant Listener mail, plus a lot of hate letters. Generally speaking they were of the "how dare you imply that all the Irish do is drink?" variety, but the hate letters were unspeakable, and I was absolutely sick about them. I was so new at this sort of thing that I answered every single letter that was signed. (And not many *are* signed. Mostly, haters like to be anonymous.) I was positive that my career was ruined, that I'd alienated all the Irish and that nobody would ever again hire me.

I know I have already mentioned crank mail, which is not to be confused with the genuine, thoughtful criticism which any performer should be grateful to get, because if somebody goes to all the trouble of analyzing what you say, it shows they're paying attention, and what could be a greater compliment? But sometimes you get angry denunciations even when you yourself haven't said anything. I've reached the conclusion that people only hear what they wish to hear, or what they expect to hear.

On my radio interview program, for example, guests are free to express their opinions—that, in fact, is why they are invited—and should I have somebody who is friendly to the Soviet Union or the Republic of China, I'm going to hear about *that,* you can bet! Never mind that I have said nothing more than "You don't say?" "What do you know!" and other noncommittal interjections, my mail is going to contain letters which tell me that I'm a rotten commy spy, a pervert, a Jew-bastard or a Jewlover (which in that type of mail are the same thing) and ask me why I don't go back where I came from. Well, Boston is a lovely place, but I don't think any useful purpose will be served by my going back there.

As an illustration that people only hear what they want to, I was amused one day when my fellow panelist on "What's My Line?", Dorothy Kilgallen, called to tell me that her mother had been to the beauty parlor and had heard two women discussing me in a neighboring booth.

They were talking about what I suppose you could call my trademark, a diamond heart which I always wear on a chain around my neck. Mrs. Kilgallen was staggered when she heard one of the women say, "Well, my dear, I found out all about that heart Arlene Francis wears. It's a hearing aid."

The other woman gasped and oohed and aahed, and Mrs. Kilgallen stood it about as long as she could before she presented herself at the entrance to their booth.

"Excuse me," she said, "I don't like to interrupt you, but I couldn't help overhearing what you were saying, and as I am Dorothy Kilgallen's mother, I happen to know that you are mistaken about that heart."

The woman listened patiently, and then in one of those maddeningly knowing tones which people affect when they think they have inside information, she said, "No, you're wrong. I know it for a fact. It *is*, believe me, a hearing aid."

Now Mrs. Kilgallen began to burn, and she said, "Why should I believe *you*? I've known her for years, and I promise you, that heart is, well, just sort of an amulet, a good luck charm. I *remember* when her husband gave it to her as an anniversary gift!"

The woman kept shaking her head, smiling tolerantly, and in the most patronizing accents she said, "My dear woman, I have it straight from the cousin of the man who created it for her!"

Mrs. K. doesn't give up easily, but no amount of arguing could change that woman's mind; that Dorothy and I had worked cheek by jowl for years and that Dorothy was the kind of person who had very sharp antennae—none of that meant anything to her. "You know how deaf people are, Mrs. Kilgallen," she said. "They never want anyone to know."

I debated, when I heard the story, about whether on the

next show I oughtn't to hold the heart in front of me at some point and say, "What was that you said, John?" and I still regret that I didn't do it. It would have made that woman's evening!

A few weeks after that episode, I took over Jack Paar's show, "Tonight," for a short spell while he was on vacation, and I told the story, and behold! A day or so later I had a letter from a man who wrote, "My wife and I heard you on that Jack Paar show, and my wife is very hard of hearing. I wondered if you would tell me where you got that hearing aid so I can get one for her?"

There is still another kind of mail which one receives—love letters. I think every performer gets some, unless you're a double for King Kong, and for all I know he gets some too from yearning female gorillas. (I had quite a nice animal following myself, come to think of it. A Scottie from Rochester always signed with a paw print and even sent me a locket with some hair in it!)

Some letters are obscene, and those you just toss into the garbage, but there are others which cause you to reflect about the desperately lonely people who fall in love with an image on the screen or a voice on the air. Think of having to reach out to strangers for affection!

Of course we are not really strangers to such people; they see us in their homes, and we become part of their lives. As with Dominick, the cab-driver with whom I started this book, they feel they have the right to call us by our first names, to advise on what we should wear, to offer suggestions concerning our careers, and I think perhaps they *do* have that right.

Love letters, therefore, would seem to be the ultimate extension of that feeling of personal involvement, and I've even had some which were proposals of marriage (in addition to the other proposals, the ones I mentioned as winding up in the garbage pail). In the event anyone supposes these letters are all written by illiterates or morons, it just isn't so. I've had some which waxed positively lyrical—as for instance:

Dearest Arlene:
I wish I could make this a beautiful letter: I wish it could be as beautiful as the feeling I have within me. I wish I could describe all the serenity, torment, loneliness and innocence, without losing the

beauty of all these things, the way they are separately and combined. It's because I love you so terribly much that I can experience opposite feelings at once. . . .

It went on at great length in that same vein, became graphic in parts, and there were poems enclosed which were dedicated to me as well. The effect this letter had on me was to make me feel terribly uncomfortable, because obviously, albeit unwittingly, I had been the cause of anguish and despair; the woman who wrote it made that quite clear.

My radio career continued at a hectic pace, and I suppose you could call me overemployed, but the busier I was, the better I liked it. I never gave my health a thought, and it never occurred to me that I ought to husband my energy. One interpretation might be that I wanted to be so busy that I wouldn't have time to think about my marriage—but that was not the entire story, by any means. I worked hard because I loved what I was doing, and it never seemed important to sit down and rest from time to time.

One of the shows that kept me bouncing around was something called "Forty-five Minutes from Hollywood," and the title was literally true. We performed forty-five minutes of a current movie, and though I am on record as saying that there was never enough time to study a character in radio acting, this program was the exception which proved the rule. Most of the stars I had to play were fairly easily impersonated women such as Bette Davis, Lupe Velez and Katharine Hepburn, all of whom had famous speech characteristics. But straight, unaccented speech was difficult. I'd sit through the picture we were going to extract from five or six times in order to study the actress I was going to play. I minded how she moved her body, what her facial characteristics were, how she held her head. (Did you know that Constance Bennett never moved her upper lip when she spoke? There, you see? That fact affected all the cadences of her delivery.)

When I had to impersonate Bette Davis in *Of Human Bondage,* I asked the director if I could have some props to work with because we were doing the scene in which Davis tears the place apart, pulling pictures off the wall and performing general mayhem. "It's *radio,* Arlene," he said.

"I know," I replied, "but I can't play it unless I'm in action. If I have to pant, I want to be really out of breath."

We had to get permission from the prop man, because around radio studios the union says he is the only one allowed to handle effects. He said okay, and a table was put up piled high with telephone books. During that particular part of the show, the studio audience was very busy dodging great chunks of pages which I threw in my fury, and the poor sponsor sat in the control booth praying he wouldn't be sued. Fortunately I didn't maim anyone. I did have one bad moment when I saw a belligerent-looking man, or I *thought* he was, heading toward me when the program was over, carrying quite a large piece of the Yellow Pages. "Would you mind autographing this?" he asked, and I was so relieved I wrote, "You've got my number, love, Arlene." He never called!

The 1943 radio version of "Blind Date" was another program which depended on "personality" and on my capacity to be spontaneous, rather than on my following a script. There too I sometimes got a little *too* spontaneous.

I must explain that among the hangovers I have carried along with me from my days at Mount St. Vincent's Academy is something the nuns pounded into me, that vulgarity is distasteful. I have to admit that with the nuns, vulgarity could mean patent leather Mary-Janes, but nevertheless I still cannot bring myself to say anything scatological, and smarmy little obscenities are simply not my style. Which doesn't mean that I am shocked or offended when I hear them, and very often I think they're terribly funny even if I can't bring myself to repeat them. If I *were* offended, I'd have to move out of the twentieth century and give up a great many of my friends.

All this being true, it is a special bit of irony that what people seem to remember about me on "Blind Date" was a salacious ad-lib. It has gone down in the annals of radio bloopers along with Uncle Don, who had been the patron saint of the kiddy shows, and his famous goof when he thought the microphones were turned off: "Go to sleep, you little bastards." It just about ruined his career, as I remember, sullying as it did the benign image of a jolly uncle.

"Blind Date" was done in a theater before an audience. As it had started during World War II, the contestants were men in various branches of the service competing for beautiful girls (aren't all girls beautiful?) who were young actresses or models. There were two men for every girl on the show, and the stage was divided so that the sexes couldn't see each other, and could only communicate through a telephone arrangement. Two boys would vie for the same girl, and she would make her selection on the basis of his voice or his conversation.

Many a night we found ourselves with a problem—particularly when the show graduated to TV later in its run—about the crestfallen look and the note of disappointment in a girl's voice when she saw she'd chosen Don Doubleugly over Tom Terrific. The prizes weren't very important or elaborate, but everybody who appeared on the show got some token, and the matched couples got a night on the town. They went to the legendary Stork Club and I went with them, either as a bonus or as a chaperone, I'm not sure which. Anyway it was all good clean fun, and there were overtones of patriotism, which, of course, was what we were trying for, though not too blatantly.

Time Magazine gave us a high rating, remarking on the spontaneous ad-lib quality of the show, and they mentioned that an exuberant sailor who had received a consolation prize of fifteen dollars had grabbed the mike and said, "Hello Clive! Set 'em up down there!" and I had grabbed it back and said, "He means Maxwell House Coffee, of course!" While this may not rank with the great humorous interpolations of all time, I mentioned it particularly to point up how sensitive all of us in that medium were. Liquor was a tsk-tsk, along with s-x, on a long list of things we were not permitted to talk about.

It was in this atmosphere, then, of high moral rectitude, that a nervous soldier, visibly shaken, stood across the microphone from me one night. He was home on leave, wearing a chestful of decorations, but wishing, I'm sure, that he was back on the battlefield rather than on television. My job was to put him at his ease, so I talked to him in as comfortable and natural a way as I could manage, but I could see he was still a-quiver. Commenting on his ribbons, I finally said, "There's no reason for you to be nervous, you've had a very good war— you've even got a purple heart on!"

On my honor, I hadn't a clue that I had said anything unusual, and I went right on with the program, thinking that the people who were laughing so hard were enjoying the poor soldier's plight, and I thought they were particularly unkind.

After the show, when the hysteria settled down in the control room, I was told that my announcement of that decoration had come out sounding like the street expression, "a purple hard-on." If *you* don't get it so much the better. I didn't either, but those times were very different, and I could have been presumed not to have known such expressions without being thought of as retarded.

My innocence in these matters led me into other traps of a similar nature, for clearly if one is ignorant in certain areas, there is no censor to tell you what pitfalls to avoid. One such circumstance occurred when a man whose hands were shaking terribly prompted me to suggest he put them in his pocket. When he had done so, with a great deal of solicitude in my tone, I asked, "Now have you got hold of yourself?"

And I suppose this also ranks with my four-star *double entendre* bloopers. Clifton Fadiman moderated a panel which consisted of those two great wits George Kaufman, Abe Burrows and me. The idea behind the show was that we three constituted an advisory board, in a sense, for people who were professionals in the entertainment business, but who felt they had some handicap or other which was holding them back.

On one show, Joan Diener came before our panel. (Later, Miss Diener made a name for herself in *Man of La Mancha*, but at the time she was relatively unknown.) When she came on stage, she positively dazzled the audience with the most magnificent set of pectoral muscles seen abroad in years. When the audience had quieted down, she stated her problem, which had to do with the fact that producers often asked her to go to supper after a rehearsal, and she felt that if she accepted, she would be too tired the next day to study properly, whereas if she didn't accept, she might antagonize the producer, and what ought she to do?

Mr. Fadiman turned to me and said, "Arlene, can you help with this?"

I pondered only a moment and replied, "Well, it seems to me that Miss Diener has *two* problems. . . ." I never got any further because the audience exploded!

■

My claim that I'd been terribly lucky—that I had a knack of being in the right place at the right time—was borne out by my having a part to play on "Big Sister" on the day that Alice Frost (the lead) was asked by her husband to help him find an actress who could do a Spanish accent.

Her husband, a casting director, worked for George Abbott, and the play they were casting was called *All That Glitters*, by John Baragwanath where the principal character is a (here we go again) hooker from South America who successfully breaks into New York Society, passing herself off as a lady of quality. The actress they were seeking had to be able to maintain a Spanish accent for three acts, and Alice set it up for me to audition for Mr. A.

Now *that* was really a dream come true, for I had haunted the office of the fabulous playwright-director-producer, as had hundreds and hundreds of other young hopefuls over the years, for exactly such a chance. It was a routine. You'd come in, wave an over-friendly hand at the receptionist and call out, "Anything today for a blonde?" "A sultry redhead?" "A seventeen-year-old ingenue?" and try not to look too anxious, but believe me, anxious is what you were. (That method of casting is over with, finished. It's all done with agents, and I suppose it's more efficient, but it isn't nearly as much fun.) At any rate, I'd never gotten near Mr. Abbott up to that point, and here suddenly I was, striding up to that same receptionist and saying, "I'm Arlene Francis," and she, *mirabile dictu,* said, "Oh yes, Miss Francis, Mr. A. is expecting you. You may go right in." I could feel the glare of pure hate searing my back from my erstwhile colleagues who were sitting around the office.

All That Glitters was not my first play, but it was my first leading role, and I think even a more seasoned actress would have been very set-up about the notices I received. They were anywhere from good to stupendous, and they reinforced my feeling that the *stage* was my milieu, and that everything else I did was just marking time.

The notices were equally good for another show I did during that period, Maxwell Anderson's *Journey to Jerusalem*. In one easy leap I'd gone from playing a prostitute to playing the Virgin Mary (with a few catcalls from so-called friends), and if anyone thinks *that* was a miracle, my Son the Messiah was played by Sidney Lumet (now one of our most prestigious directors of motion pictures), whose job just before that had been as a hoodlum, one of the original *Dead End* kids in the play of that name by Sidney Kingsley. (And I will ask everyone kindly to remember that Mary was in her early teens when Jesus was born!)

I did several plays, most of them somewhat less than memorable, but all of them had respectable runs and a respectable press at the time. (Nowadays, it is almost impossible for a play which is less than a tremendous smash to survive the killing economics of the Broadway theater, but then plays could go along for quite a long time without being standing-room-only successes. It was a far healthier theater, I believe.) The casts of the plays I did invariably included actors and actresses who were very glamorous to me, because their careers had been exclusively in the theater. That put me in awe of them, no matter how much more money I was making in radio than they could make in the theater. I think most of us who had gotten our start in radio felt that way, that people in the theater were special. Radio was meat and potatoes, but the theater was caviar. And it was always flattering (and it still is) when theater people would come backstage, as they sometimes did, to congratulate me on a performance. Wouldn't any actress be thrilled to have an aging Katharine Cornell, not in the most robust health, come climbing up a long flight of stairs to praise a performance, as I must shamelessly admit she did after seeing me in *Mrs. Dally*. It implied acceptance of me as a colleague, and was a greater accolade in my mind than even a good notice.

Inevitably, as a result of those notices, there were several feature articles about me in newspapers and magazines. There were pictures of me in our "lavish" Park Avenue apartment and on our "palatial" Southbury estate. Public relations people tend to refer to anything which is not actually a lean-to as an "estate," but it *is* true that our farm up in Southbury was uncommonly pretty and had a lot of acreage on which there were some stables and lakes. It embarrassed me, however, to be made to sound like landed gentry, when all I really wanted was a small plot of ground, the size of a stage, to act upon.

I had such a heavy schedule during this period of my life that one would have thought I wouldn't have had time for a

12. With Joe Cotten in *Horse Eats Hat* (and quite a mouthful—the hat, that is).
13. Orson Welles directing me and Joe Cotten in *Horse Eats Hat*.
14. With Sidney Lumet in *Journey to Jerusalem* (The Virgin *who?*).
15. With one of my devoted admirers.
16. *The Doughgirls*—and back to the hospital at night (after my bows of course!).

11

12   13

16

14   15

private life. Well sir, one would have been dead wrong. It was so private that I didn't dare mention it to anyone in the world, but it certainly existed. What had happened was that I had fallen in love with Martin.

It kept me awake nights worrying, for Martin kept urging me to make a clean break with Neil. He felt it would be more honorable and decent and all that, and he made the point that I was prolonging the agony by putting it off, and that there was no point in making three people unhappy. I agreed in theory, but I simply hadn't the courage to do that to Neil. I can't imagine what I thought would happen if I asked him for a divorce. What ridiculous egos we have, for that is really what it is no matter what we tell ourselves! I thought it would be the end for Neil if I left him.

In order to avoid thinking about it at all, I took on more and more jobs and worked harder than ever. Personal appearances at a ladies' club? Delighted. New role in a soap opera? With pleasure. Fly to Butte, Montana, to present an award? Why not? Do a commercial? Of course. Queen of a festival? Honored. And to top everything off, in 1942 I was offered one of the leads in a comedy by Joseph Fields, called *The Doughgirls*.

I loved the play, loved my part, and was thrilled that it would be directed by George S. Kaufman. It was quite a coup for me, and I hoped I would be so absorbed in what I was doing on stage, I would be able to toss my private woes out the window.

We went into rehearsal, and I took Russian accent lessons at the same time, for I was playing a Russian girl sniper, patterned loosely on the Soviet heroine of the war, Ludmilla Pavlechenko, who had captured everyone's imagination by being a one-woman brigade. I was certainly busy, but not too busy to do what any red-blooded, fun-loving American girl with money, success, fame and a doting husband would do: I went off and had me a nervous breakdown.

5

Actually it was only a mini-breakdown, if there is such a thing. I didn't go climbing walls or fall into a stupor, but it was noted that I had been losing weight, with no apparent reason behind such a loss, and that I seemed depressed and a bit hollow-eyed. In addition, I was frequently fretful and short-tempered, which was really quite unusual for me, and nobody could find any physical reason for any of these things. At Neil's and my parents' insistence I had a thorough check-up, and the doctor suggested that I go into a hospital for observation.

Considering the rigors of my work schedule, it was not difficult for anyone to believe that I was on the verge of collapse from overwork, that I had been doing too many things and driving myself too hard. I agreed to the hospital, but I flatly refused to give up my role in *The Doughgirls* while they were "observing" me, so I was a live-in patient at a small private hospital called the LeRoy Sanitarium, which meant that I was allowed to leave for performances, but I had to come back to sleep. It was a little bit like being a prison trusty, but the food was somewhat better.

Neil believed completely in the "overworked" theory, for I had successfully hidden from him the fact that I had any emotional turmoil, and *that* I consider to have been the best performance I ever gave in my life. He was convinced that I'd be all right as soon as I'd had a good rest, and he kept at me, trying to make me promise I'd cut down on my activities where work was concerned. Each day he'd arrive at the hospital with flowers or perfume or a silly gift, have lunch with me, and try to make me laugh. I'd look at him and say to myself, "Why can't you be an s.o.b. like other girls' husbands?" and I'd try to laugh at his jokes and wind up crying at my dilemma, as he tried to comfort me.

I had one very good friend who knew that what was troubling me was a good deal more than fatigue. His name was Fred Uttal, and he was an announcer who had been on several shows I'd acted in. We had more than the usual working camaraderie, however, because he owned a farm in Southbury across from ours, so we spent time together on weekends and had become close and warm friends. His mother was a good friend too, and I think they must have talked me over and decided that I needed a bit of help. Mrs. Uttal knew a psychoanalyst named Dr. Arnold Hutschnecker on a social basis, and she asked him if he'd look in on me at the hospital, just on a friendly basis in a very informal way, and she must have made it sound quite urgent because he did come to see me, although it isn't the sort of thing psychoanalysts do!

Dr. Hutschnecker probed around into my psyche so gently that I didn't even know that was what he was doing, for the thought would never have occurred to me in a million years that I might be in need of psychiatric guidance. I'd been brought up to believe that people had an obligation to deal with their own problems as best they could, and that calling upon psychiatrists for help was a sign of weakness. This was really a strange outlook, because I am talking about an era in which polite conversation consisted of discussions of everyone's id and libido, and most of my neurotic friends (is there any other kind?) were trundling their way up Park Avenue daily to visit their doctors and have them analyze their dreams. It seemed, in my uneducated view, to be self-indulgent, and I would have had none of it had it not been for the "steering" of wise Dr. Hutschnecker. He never became my doctor, but I did feel he was my friend, and he made it possible for me to consider psychiatric treatment to help me solve my problems. Eventually I found a doctor of my own, and in due time I found the courage to change my life around.

Meanwhile, back at the Lyceum Theater, *The Doughgirls* had become a solid smash. It was immensely funny, "dandy escapist comedy" as one critic called it, "loaded with laughter" according to another, and it was apparently just what the country wanted and needed to cheer it up in the middle of the war.

Talk about your schizoid existences, though. As Natalya Chodorov (my name in the play, a tribute from Mr. Fields to his collaborator on other plays, Jerry Chodorov, who was serving in the army at the time), I stamped around the stage with a sixty-pound dog under my arm, my back in a brace, my feet in heavy boots, and a rifle slung over my shoulder. I had most of the laugh lines, and according to the critics, I didn't let Mr. Fields or Mr. Kaufman down, but every night I'd pack up my laughs and put them away, pick up my suitcase full of worries and take it back to the hospital and unpack it.

In some ways I was living out a good old theatrical tradition, the essence of show business, or what people associate with show business—laugh, clown, laugh. The real phenomenon was that as long as I was actually inside the theater, working on stage or clowning around with members of the cast or crew backstage, in a rather roguish trick of the mind, I was able to forget about the hospital and my private concerns entirely. It was as though they had agreed to lurk back there in never-never land and not bother me while I was performing.

So completely did they stay in the background that I was able to participate in, and sometimes even to initiate, the special kind of lunacy that goes on backstage when a company has been together for a while. You begin to have family jokes, of a sort, and to play tricks on each other (unless you all happen to hate each other, which is also a possibility). We liked each other in *The Doughgirls,* and if you don't think that's remarkable, bear in mind that the four leading characters were women, of whom three, at least, were sensational looking—Virginia Fields, Doris Nolan and Arleen Whelan—and normally competitive. Thus there was a real potential for bitchiness and elbow-jogging for a share of the limelight, but it never developed, and I can't remember even a mildly unpleasant occurrence. Matter of fact, there was another *Doughgirls'* beauty in a supporting role, Mary Cooper, who became at that time and remains to this day a very dear friend indeed. Yes, we all got on famously.

Doris and I shared a dressing room upstairs, and Arleen and Virginia were at stage level (no status was involved—we tossed a coin)—so naturally people coming backstage to see us after a performance would stop at their dressing room first. This riled Doris and me because sometimes they stayed so long, they never made it upstairs, and we proclaimed loudly that it was all owing to Arleen's gorgeous red hair which so dazzled callers that they were held spellbound.

We announced to the female members of the cast that we, Doris and I, were going to do a private entertainment for their benefit on Valentine's day. We then took ourselves to a hairdressing establishment where I knew the woman in charge. She hustled us into a small room in the rear, when I made known our wants, and we stripped for a bleach and dye on what we privately called our public hair, and then cut it in the shape of a heart. Now I am an absolute dark brunette no matter what I look like on top, and there was such a howling and screaming while I was being dyed, that clients in the main room must have thought we were having root canal work performed without Novocaine. But anything for art. Before the matinee, while various ladies of the ensemble watched (no men were invited, you may be sure), we appeared, kimono-draped, recited a poem we B girls had written about the girls in Dressing Room A, and at the last line we flashed our Valentines for a dynamite finish. We were a sensation. I, in fact, was a sensation twice. Once on the stage, and once when I got back to the hospital and repeated the performance for the nurses on my floor.

The hospital tests having given me a clean bill of health physically, I went into treatment with the late Dr. Herman Nunberg, a renowned and remarkable psychoanalyst, and with his help I gained the strength I needed to strike out on my own—to actually move bag and baggage out of the house. But even at that, I so dreaded the thought of a possible scene that I snuck out like a thief in the night, leaving a letter for Neil. I simply wasn't up to doing it on a face-to-face basis. I remember checking into the Hampshire House and sitting on the bed in my room, waiting for him to call, which I was sure he would do as soon as he had read my note, and which of course is exactly what he did. As anyone can imagine, his bewilderment was total. In all this time he had had no clue that I was anything but a contented wife, however overworked I might be—and to get a note like that out of the blue! But admirable as always, there was not even a hint of recrimination in his tone as he asked me if we might not have dinner and discuss the situation. I agreed, of course.

Having made the actual physical break, it was easier for me than I had thought to explain to Neil some of what I felt, what I had been feeling for so long a time. Not all, of course. There were areas which I couldn't discuss even then, which would be too hurtful to him, I felt. I saw him fairly often, and he courted me as though we had just met, but I was building up strengths which enabled me to resist not only his blandishments (including a lovely little house which he bought in New York as an enticement to get me to change my mind) but those of my parents, who also would have given anything to see me go back to the status which had been quo.

There was not the slightest possibility of that. For one thing, I actually adored living in the little apartment I'd finally rented on Central Park South. I'd never had a place of my own, for I'd gone from my parents' house to Neil's, and looking back, it seems to me that if I had had a little more time then to be a young woman alone, free to make choices, really to grow up internally as well as externally, things could conceivably have been different. I don't think everything that has happened with the younger generation is necessarily an improvement over mine, but one thing I do approve is the move among young people to strike out on their own when they feel that they are equipped to do that (provided that they really are, of course). "Nice" girls didn't move away from the protection of their parents' roofs in my day (I hate that phrase!), especially when those parents were as uncompromisingly old-fashioned as were mine.

They, by the way, were harder for me to deal with than Neil was. I found myself constantly consoling them as though they had lost a son—which was not too far from being true. There was one point where Neil and I happened both to be in California at the same time on our respective jobs, and naturally we saw each other often. Because my parents seem to have saved every scrap of paper I ever wrote on, I ran across a letter I sent them at that time, which said in part,

Neil and I have had a lot of evenings together and I tried with all my heart to find out if we could make a go of it again. We have talked it all out and had it in the open and my Juarez divorce has been arranged. I know this is very distressing to you both, but I tried—for *your* sakes I tried, but I cannot live my life through you, as deeply as I love you. He is a splendid man and all is warm and friendly between us.

There is just one thing I want you to do for me because I know you want me to keep this healthy happiness I have gained. When I come back, let us never discuss this. Please, because you care, let me keep what has torn me apart for so long entirely to myself. I implore you not to cry, for if it is really I who matters in your hearts, it is a time for rejoicing. My aching has dropped from me and left me a girl I forgot I once was. . . . I love you both forever. . . .

The Juarez divorce took half an hour, if that, and I couldn't help feeling that there was something shabby about ending a relationship between a man and a woman in this brief, clinical way.

Neil, by the way, did not jump out of the window or throw himself in front of a moving vehicle. He went to Paris, met a lovely woman and married her. So much for my ego trip.

(He did die an untimely death, but it had nothing to do with me. It had to do with a respiratory ailment, and when he died in a hospital in Boston, his French wife, not knowing the complicated formalities which survivors must go through, and feeling terribly alone and bewildered, got in touch with me for help. I called Spyros Skouras, and I shall never forget his kindness, his decency. Though he had not seen Neil in years, he leaped in and took charge of everything.)

The attachment which my parents had felt for Neil made it very rough for Martin, needless to say. He was a lot of things they couldn't get used to: an actor, a man whose entire professional life was bound up in the theater as a director and producer as well, and he was Jewish. All of these things were all *right* to be, if you should ask them, but of course you wouldn't want your only daughter, etc., etc., etc.

Neither Mother nor Daddy would ever dream of saying such things aloud, of course, but Martin felt them hanging over him like the sword of Damocles. If he could have brought himself to be a little more deferential or pacifying, perhaps he could have won them over—or so I used to believe at the time. Actually, his behavior was beyond reproach, for Martin is the soul of courtesy. But he is also a man of great pride, and if "winning them over" implied that he must kow-tow or grovel, then they would have to remain un-won.

I'm sure my parents would have vigorously denied that there was any tinge of anti-Semitism in their feelings about Martin, but they spoke of "mixed" marriages with great mis-givings, which was pretty funny, all things considered, as they were pretty "mixed" themselves. An Armenian Greek-Ortho-dox Catholic and an Anglo-Saxon Protestant, so what was the big deal? "Well," they would argue, "what about if you have a child?" "Well, what about it?" I wanted to know. "Poor thing," they would reply, "it wouldn't know what it was."

To skip ahead a bit, as everyone who has ever been within the sound of my voice knows, eventually we did produce a child, and "poor thing" knows exactly what "it" is. *It* is Peter Gabel, superior human being. Religion never loomed as an issue so far as I am concerned, although I must admit that Martin sometimes has a tendency to get somewhat dramatic about being a Jew, and is given to speaking of "My people" with great emotion.

Martin had a "My people" episode when Peter was reach-ing for his twelfth birthday, and he decided that he ought really to be Bar Mitzvah when he was thirteen, which meant that something ought to be done about his religious training. Now, according to the Jews, Peter isn't even Jewish because religion is matrilinearly determined. (A very realistic point of view, I think, since there's certainly never any doubt about the *maternity* of a child.) But according to me and Martin, Peter is at least half Jewish, and I say "at least" because I cannot guar-antee that I never had a Jewish forebear. Who can? In any case, it was okay with me about the Bar Mitzvah, my only con-dition being that Martin should see to all the arrangements. A girl who went to a Presbyterian Sunday School and was gradu-ated from a Catholic Convent shouldn't be asked to take on chores she doesn't understand.

Ah, but being dramatic about being a Jew, member of a gallant and tragic people and all that, didn't necessarily mean that you knew anything about going to a synagogue, nor that you were prepared to sit with your son and cue him on those "Today I am a man" lines. The result was that Peter never did get all those wonderful pen and pencil sets, and that he will have to make it to heaven on his own, without rabbi, priest, minister or druid to intercede for him. So far as I am concerned, he'll make it in a walk.

There has only been one occasion when religion was discussed on any level between Peter and myself. He was about six years old, and he came home from school one day and said, "Mom, you're not Jewish, are you?"

"No," I said, very puzzled. "Why do you ask?"

"But Dad and I *are*, right?"

I shrugged. "If you say so, darling, that's okay."

He shook his head. "No, it's not okay."

Thoroughly bewildered, I asked, "Why isn't it?"

"Because," he replied with great earnestness, "If you were Jewish, you wouldn't have to go to the studio tomorrow. It's Rosh Hashonoh."

As anyone can see, already a theological wonder was Peter Gabel, Armenian-English-Austrian-Russian-Polish-Greek Orthodox-Protestant Jew. In other words, your typical American boy.

Oh yes, there was one other occasion upon which Peter exhibited his religious know-how. His nurse, a Catholic, asked my permission to take him along with her to Mass at St. Patrick's Cathedral one Sunday morning, and I agreed. It was a special occasion of some kind, and His Eminence, Cardinal Spellman (at the time Archbishop Spellman) stood at the door when the celebrants left the church. He patted Peter on the head and said, "God bless you," at which Peter looked up gravely surprised and said, "I didn't sneeze!"

I did not, incidentally, rush from the divorce court into Martin's arms and wedding bells. All that newfound freedom was very exciting to me, and I was reluctant to give it up too quickly. Besides, now that I could see Martin openly, there didn't seem to me to be any great urgency about making it a permanent status. Martin couldn't have been more understanding and gentle about it.

A shade too understanding, it began to appear to me. I mean, why wasn't he bludgeoning me? Why wasn't he sending down ultimata? Indeed, how did it happen that he casually announced to me that he was going off to California, without even a sinister hint about the bikini-clad beauties of Burbank?

The reason he was going was to be co-producer with Walter Wanger of a motion picture starring Susan Hayward, called *Smash-Up,* and he would be gone for a few months. We spoke to each other fairly often during the time that he was away, but I began to brood a little about all those terrific starlets who were reputed to be so very, well, available to producers. Nothing is as dangerous to a long distance relationship as an available starlet.

And so, when Martin came to New York to get a second unit of the picture into production, I lost no time letting him know that I was ready to get married. "Excellent," he said, smiling smugly, and off we went to get our Wassermans. (Passed them, too, I'm happy to report.)

We went to the Stork Club that night to celebrate with Martin's closest friend and his wife, Lou Calhern and Marianne Stewart. Rhea and Jerry Chodorov and Jimmy Cannon, the great sportswriter and another of Martin's cronies, joined us at our table, and what with one toast and another, the news of our impending nuptials spread around the club very quickly, so that soon we were testing our capacity to consume champagne which was sent to us by well-wishers, and doing very well, thank you. Our table got joined to other tables, and we began to resemble one of those Italian wedding parties you see in films by Fellini, except this was pre-marital, and that reminded somebody: When was the wedding to be? We weren't sure. Where was it to be? We didn't know. The problem was that Mexican divorces weren't recognized at that time in New York, so we would have to go out of the state.

Walter Winchell, patron saint of the Stork Club, had become a member of our party by then, and he said not to worry. When Winchell said not to worry in those days, you didn't dare worry. He had this friend who was a judge in Paterson, New Jersey, who would marry us. Well, we welled, but what if the friend wasn't there? Winchell fixed us with a withering look and sent for a phone to be plugged in next to the table. He spoke into it briefly, hung up, and said, "He'll be there. Noon tomorrow. *You* be there."

Hangover notwithstanding, rather than risk Winchell's displeasure, the next morning we piled into a limousine, with Jimmy Cannon and Lou Calhern along to keep our spirits up and to be our witnesses, then took off for Paterson where Winchell's friend the judge married us under an intimidating picture of Alf Landon. I don't know *why* Landon's picture was there. It must have been a terribly stubborn judge who had never acknowledged the presidencies of Roosevelt or Truman, but anyway the marriage was perfectly legal. The Paterson evening paper headlined the happy event: "Arlene Francis Marries Hollywood Notable," and the Hollywood Notable wryly remarked, "If I'm such a notable," he said, "how come they don't mention my name?"

(Actually, my greater visibility has never been any issue whatever between us. Martin understands that it is the nature of the beast, TV that is, which is responsible, and he accepts it without affect because he is in no doubt about his own abilities. It is only people who are insecure who have this need to jostle to get out in front.

George S. Kaufman once told me that for all his Pulitzer prize, his spectacular career as a playwright and director-producer, the elevator man in his building was totally uninterested in him until he appeared on that game show I described, the one with Abe Burrows, Clifton Fadiman and me, on TV, where we discussed Joan Diener's mammary glands. After that it was "YesSIR, Mr. Kaufman, Harrya, Mr. Kaufman, everything okay, Mr. Kaufman?" all the way.)

Considering the problems we'd had getting to this state—the tortured romance, the clandestine meetings and teary farewells, our agonized soul-searching and my nervous breakdown—considering all that, the scenario called for us to gaze tenderly at each other and ignore the rest of the world as the nuptial limousine sped into the sunrise to the happy ending. Instead, guess who got ignored as the groom and his two attendants rehashed a big prize-fight of the previous week?

Yes indeed. The conversation, as I remember it, on MY WEDDING DAY, mind you, consisted largely of "If he'da give him his right to the jaw, it'a been all over!" and more in that vein.

I have just realized that most of the people I have talked about who are connected in my mind to our wedding are dead: Susan Hayward, Walter Wanger, Lou Calhern, Jimmy Cannon, Walter Winchell, Roosevelt, Truman. Thank goodness the Chodorovs, Marianne, Martin and I have made it so far. And as of this writing, so has Alf Landon. I'm not sure about the judge.

6

There were many things I had to get used to about Martin. One of the things I had always admired about him, been terribly proud of in fact, was that he was so very well informed. But as well as I knew him, even *I* hadn't quite realized what a staggering amount of information he had in such areas as history, the theater, poetry, the sporting world, literature, semantics and so on and so on. (He has also asked me to include in this list, which I have of course shown him, the fact that he has a not inconsiderable flair for handicapping horses. *Flair* is the word I have chosen, although he objects to it, quoting somebody who said, "A man with a flair is a man who *guesses* what he ought to *know*." Martin contends that he *knows* his horseflesh.)

Now then, you take a girl who was finished at Finch and stack her up against a man with that kind of erudition and what have you got? A well-stacked girl who sometimes feels pretty ignorant. Or at least I did in the beginning, because since then I've met so many smart people, interviewed them on my program, gotten to know them, and tried to let as much as possible rub off on me. But even though I'm not as bad as I used to be, I still have a tendency to slink into a corner when Martin starts a conversation with "As Pliny the Elder remarked . . ."

Martin used to think this diffidence on my part concerning his vast store of information was an elaborate put-on, and when he realized that it wasn't, he got to work trying to help me get over it. I've already told about the incident where he heard me express myself on the subject of Senator McCarthy, his pleased surprise that I spoke up where it counted, so to speak. Among his methods for helping to build my confidence was his use of psychological shock treatment. He'd make jokes about it, hoping I'd see how silly I was. "Look at her," he'd say, "poor little thing. I married beneath me, you know. She used to wear a fur hat and muff and fringe on her skirt—hadn't a clue about style!" Or on a serious level he would enumerate the pluses: my public acceptance, the demand for me in jobs, the gratifying number of very good friends and so on, trying to force me into a modicum of self-confidence. And through the years (for this condition is a persistent one) he has never missed an opportunity to say something gracious on both private and public occasions. I burst into tears, for instance, when on our twenty-eighth wedding anniversary, he toasted me by saying, "I feel as though I am not so much a husband as the custodian of a national treasure!" And when he accepted his "Tony" award for *Big Fish, Little Fish,* he said, "This is the first thing I've won since Arlene Francis consented to be my wife!"

I have gone to some lengths to describe this quirk in my personality, because it was something which first came into full flower during that interim period between my divorce and my remarriage—when Martin took me around to meet his friends, and I became aware that there was a whole world full of people who knew things that I knew very little about. I don't mean friends such as Lou Calhern or Jimmy Cannon—they were as much part of my world as they were of Martin's and they didn't intimidate me in the least. I am talking about the bright, brittle group of notables who gathered around Herbert Bayard Swope. *They* scared me.

The Swopes ran a unique household. It is not enough to call it a salon, for it bore a closer resemblance to a fiefdom, with Herbert and his dowager-duchess-type wife Maggie, as the feudal lords. It wasn't that they were so very rich—indeed, compared to *really* rich people they counted themselves paupers. Although Herbert had, at one time, amassed a great fortune, he had lost the bulk of it in the stock market crash of '29. He was left with a piddling million or so, which was a lot of money from some vantage points (mine, for instance), but not enough to run the kind of place they ran. All of his friends speculated about how they managed to employ all those servants, people who unpacked for you, who pressed your clothes, who did your laundry, who brought you breakfast in bed, who washed your money, and who filled the tank of your car with gasoline from the Swopes' private tank before you left on Monday morning after you had spent the weekend. Nobody could figure out how they did it.

If you can imagine a perpetual house party, with twelve or fourteen guest rooms always filled and forty sitting down to dinner as the norm, that's what it was like at the Swopes'. And what a forty! To be asked there was an acknowledgment that you were the peer of the nation's most impressive literary, social, journalistic, theatrical or political figures. Martin is far from shy about what he knows and what his capabilities are, but even he was a bit overwhelmed by the esteem in which the Swopes held him. He was one of the "regulars," and they were so fond of him that they frequently urged him to move in bag and baggage and be part of the household.

Herbert had started his career as a journalist in Kansas City, had come east to be a reporter on the old New York *World,* and had risen to be its executive editor. He won a Pulitzer prize for reporting and wrote several books, but none of these things of themselves would account for the towering place he held as a figure on the New York scene. Some people are born stars, and Herbert was one of them. Neither he nor Maggie had sprung from the privileged class, but they had remedied that situation by creating a privileged class of their own—the people who were invited to be guests in their home. "We're going to the Swopes'" was one of those phrases one dropped to let everyone know they'd made it into the big time.

Dinner at the Swopes' usually included several of the neighborhood folks, but it was *some* neighborhood out there on Long Island, and they were *some* folks: among others, the Vanderbilts, the Phippses, the Whitneys, the Harrimans—and a pair of people who were woven into the fabric of our lives from almost the day we met them—George and Eve Backer. They were, to use a term Evie used to describe people *she* thought were superior human beings, "first clahss"—George, the handsome, articulate sage, and Evie, who had the greatest taste, the sharpest wit, and a prodigious capacity for friendship. (They are both, alas, gone now, and sorely missed.)

The rest of the party would include the current theater

and literary figures of the day, say, George Kaufman, Moss Hart, Dorothy Parker, George Abbott, a covey of best-selling novelists and a gaggle of statesmen (they stopped being merely "politicians" when they arrived at the Swopes' door). Noel Coward, Cole Porter, Richard and Dorothy Rodgers might be there perhaps, and if there was a Nobel scientist anywhere within commuting distance, he'd be asked and you may be sure he'd come. One could always look forward to a generous reaping of the celebrity harvest.

Of the parties we attend these days, the closest I can think of to rival those Swope parties are the ones given by Mollie Parnis. They are not three- or four-day house parties, but they certainly are gatherings of the most glittering personalities in America (and of any interesting foreigners who happen to be in town).

Mollie is, of course, the redoubtable dress designer, with hundreds of thousands of fans of her own, but among her most endearing qualities is that she is herself an unabashed fan of talent and enterprise, wherever she finds it. (By that I mean it isn't *always* celebrities who win her admiration. She initiated and has continued to sponsor a campaign in slums and ghettos called "Dress Up Your Neighborhood," and her enthusiasm for children who have made flowers grow in dump heaps is enormous—as are the rewards she metes out, because Mollie is a lady who puts her money where her mouth is. Each year she has given thousands and thousands of dollars to neighborhood dressers-upper.)

But about her parties—whether it is a huge election night party (which even the candidates don't like to miss, often sneaking away from election headquarters to check in at Mollie's), or a chic little dinner for twelve, you know it won't be just a body count or a name-harvest. All the gracious touches will be there: gourmet food, beautiful service, lovely flowers, but best of all, the right mix of people to keep things buzzing along. I've been there to hear Henry Kissinger hold forth on foreign policy and Lyndon Johnson discuss the presidency. Senators, congressmen and newspaper editors, authors, actors and ambassadors all discover each other and open up in the warm ambience of Mollie's house. I remember that one night at a very special big party, a friend leaned over to me and said, "I'm absolutely perishing to meet the mayor," and I said,

"Jerusalem or New York?" because they were both there, Teddy Kolleck and John Lindsay.

To get back to the Swopes, Herbert and Maggie had a magic quality about them. They were so beguiling that they had only to crook a finger and everyone came flying, for they knew that a party at the Swopes' would be a provocative, lively event, sparkling with brilliant conversation, dazzling wit, and all sorts of material goodies to make you feel pampered.

If you were to ask Martin what his great attraction for the Swopes was, he would shrug modestly and say, "One must not overlook the incredible power of that most prized of all guests—the extra man." Modest or no, that was partly true. To be sure, he has an enviable gift for anecdotage. He also has the kind of mind which retains little-known facts, a quality which Herbert adored because he had it himself in copious quantity, and he and Martin would match obscurities by the hour, but that extra-man thing was not to be overlooked.

It worried me, in the beginning, that the Swopes, especially Maggie, would not thank me for thinning out the ranks. Fortunately she took a liking to me, and she actually urged Martin to persuade me to make it official as quickly as possible. In spite of my social acceptance, I wish I could say that I eventually learned to feel completely at home there, but I never did. Not even after I had achieved some recognition myself as a panelist on "What's My Line?" and therefore qualified for the Swopes' definition of a *star*. I did become very, very fond of them both, and was deeply saddened by Herbert's death, and then Maggie's some years later. In addition to feeling a personal loss, it was as though a period had been affixed to a very gleaming era in New York's social history.

Martin advised me in a number of matters having to do with my career, and with business things not directly connected with my work. Usually his advice was excellent, and there was one occasion when I could have kicked myself for not listening to him. Before we were married he brought me the script of *Life With Father,* in which he and Carly Wharton, with whom he was then in partnership as a producing team, were involved. He thought I should invest in it, and after reading it I said, "If you ask me, who's going to be interested in a play about a man getting baptized?" How fortunate for Lindsay and Crouse, the authors (Howard Lindsay, of course, played the lead role as well, with his enchanting wife Dorothy Stickney as co-star), and the people who got rich on one of the longest-running shows in the history of the theater, that they *didn't* ask me.

Martin taught me a great deal about being a public person. "You must always leave the house," he said, "as though you expect to be photographed when you get to the street. Even if you only have to run down to the drugstore for aspirin, don't skate, and don't wear curlers in your hair!"

And I listened to him. After all, in sartorial matters I could hardly give short shrift to one who is acknowledged to be a member of an endangered species—a genuine dandy! Why, up until very recently, Martin refused to have celluloid tabs in his collars because he felt that a well-cut shirt didn't require them. All mechanical contrivances are anathema to him, and that includes not only bow ties on a band, but zippers on a fly. Martin is, in fact, a fop's fop, and in those rarefied circles they proudly recount the story of how he won fifty dollars from his agent and our friend, Irving Lazar, by betting that he, Irving, was the only person present who had a zipper on his trouser fly. There were four men present besides Irving and Martin, all fellow dandies, and Martin collected his fifty dollars as they proudly displayed their buttons.

Even though I didn't feel myself up to trading quips with the likes of Noel Coward, the world into which Martin brought me was one I had always longed to be part of. Neil's world, although it had been involved with entertainment, was really the business world. It might just as well have been involved with real estate, for it dealt with the financial end of the motion picture industry and certainly didn't include writers, directors and actors except on a very superficial level. But such people were the main core of Martin's world, and he used to tease me by saying, "If it weren't for me you'd still be hanging around with Balaban and Katz."

Even my parents were impressed with my new friends, especially my mother, who was as goggle-eyed as a child when it came to celebrities. Their attitude toward my marriage softened considerably when they saw how happy I was, and as time went along and they came to know Martin better, they did a complete about-face. Martin and my father developed a healthy mutual respect, an affection even, for each other. As for my mother, she became so attached to him that one would have thought she had always been his staunchest friend and ally. And after my father became ill, and most especially after his death, my mother turned to Martin for all judgments, regarding him in fact as the Rock of Gibraltar, as compared to her flibbertigibbet daughter who wouldn't have sense enough to wear her rubbers if Martin wasn't there to remind her.

It took quite a bit of time for those attitudes to develop, however, and in the beginning, before they had become reconciled to our marriage, I felt as though I were walking a tightrope between my parents and my husband. Cold politeness on both sides was the order of the day, and a fat lot of help I got from my husband! In fact, with his flawless sense of timing, he took off right after we were married, for the coast to finish *Smash-Up* and left the job of parent-pacification to me.

We had planned that I would join him as soon as I was able to wind up all my obligations in New York, a process which would take about a month. My Broadway show was closing, "Blind Date" was going off the air because the war was over and it would have to find a new formula, and I wanted to get myself written out of the other shows I had been doing. I was going to make a fresh start, and for the first time since I'd gotten my first professional job, I was completely without commitments. It was a little frightening, all things considered, to be venturing into brand new territory, with a brand new husband, to be starting a brand new life.

7

I had a sneaking suspicion right from the first that California would not be the end of the rainbow for me. It was scenically lovely, we had lots of friends, the climate was heaven, there were interesting and wonderful people out there, *but*—it became appallingly clear to me that I was now classified as A Wife, not a very elevated status in that business at that time. It wasn't Martin who was doing the classifying. It was just the condition that prevailed in the Hollywood of thirty years ago, which had to have a label to attach to you before it knew how it ought to treat you. Unless you were yourself a star, your role was that of a second-class citizen. As a wife, you were an appendage who had her work cut out for her. You ran the house, entertained, shopped, gossiped and spent your days around the pool or at luncheon with other wives, doing lots of things which might sound like Paradise, unless you had to do them all the time. I mean what's so awful about eating truffles and playing tennis? Nothing at all, unless you'd rather be working.

I wasn't Hollywood's notion of a big star. No matter that I had a tremendous radio audience because of "Blind Date" and other shows. No matter that I had played leading roles on Broadway. Hollywood had its own criteria, and a bigger bosom would have been a greater advantage than good notices where I was concerned. Or perhaps Selznick was right about my nose. Whatever the reason, nobody came battering down my door to beg me to do an epic. It didn't matter at first in any case, because I had too much to do just setting up the mechanics for living.

Before leaving for California, Glenda Farrell, a good friend who had played with me in *The Overtons* by Vincent Lawrence, had offered to lend Martin and me her house in the Valley until we could find a place of our own. I had accepted with pleasure, and indeed it was a lovely house, with only one drawback: it was just about impossible to find anyone to work in it. To me, this was a whole new ball game, and as I wrote to my mother, "It's a constant chase between the ironing board, the phone and the front door. I'm waiting now to interview a maid upon whom I will settle a rather large dowry if she will just get the beds made. . . ." I can hear small voices saying, "Too bad about her," but it should be remembered that although I had always worked very hard indeed, I had practically no familiarity with *housework,* and despite what some people think, that is *not* a skill which is automatically included with the rest of the female accoutrements. A little scouring and scrubbing went, and still goes, a long way with me!

To make matters worse, I hadn't realized that I'd married a bachelor. I don't mean somebody who had never been married, I mean somebody born to be a bachelor. He will deny this, but Martin's favorite pastimes (with a few striking exceptions) are male-oriented. Like shooting the breeze with the boys at the bar, playing a few games of pool at the Players' Club, or handicapping the races with Danny Lavezzo at a table at P. J. Clarke's, which Danny owns. Domestic bliss to Marty meant that everything was blissful as long as I was the domestic.

This realization covered me like a blanket one day when our trunks arrived from New York. Martin and Lou Calhern (another paragon among husbands, and why not, since he'd been to the post five times?) were sitting out on the terrace, laughing and scratching, while I lugged suitcases and packing crates into the house, panting every step of the way. When the job was just about finished, Martin became aware that some activity had apparently been going on behind his back, and he called out to me, "Is there anything I can do, darling?"

"Obviously not," I said through clenched teeth, "but I certainly wish I'd known that before we were married."

We must have made up, because shortly after that I discovered I was pregnant. Ecstatic at the news, Martin did a

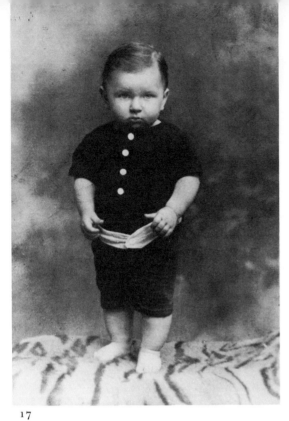

17. "Don't start up with me—I'm Big Marty from Philly."
18. Martin with his fellow bachelor Lou Calhern.
19. Harry Kurnitz, Abe Burrows and Martin discussing another Kurnitz comedy, *Reclining Figure*.
20. With Elisabeth Bergner in *Cup of Trembling*.

17
18

19

20

21. It's breeding that counts.
22. "Jesus—not another story about the Swopes, Dad!"
23. Caption by Mark Goodson for our 28th anniversary party—"And then you'll go on to the Supreme Court, darling."
24. "Being totally present"—all in the family.
25. "No, I didn't coach him. Peter *loves* Shakespeare."

21

22

23

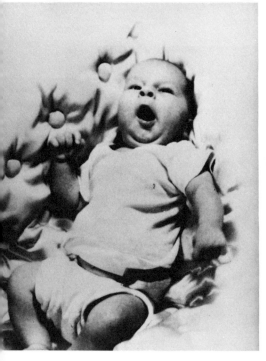

24

25

complete reversal, clucking over me, stuffing pillows behind my back when I sat down, shielding me from being jostled in a crowd, treating me generally as though I were just recovering from a major heart attack. I had to tell him that pregnancy isn't a disease, that I was in splendid health, thank you, and would he please buzz off and stop saying "Hadn't you better sit down, darling?"

I kept a steady stream of letters going to my parents, knowing how lonely they were for one reason, but for another, it was my way of telling them that I really hadn't done too badly, that I was leading a glamorous and activity-filled life. These are excerpts from a bundle of letters which they saved, all tied up in pink ribbon, and from the size of that bundle I must have found a maid or else I had the most neglected house in Southern California.

I'm going over to Walter and Joan Wanger's house this afternoon. . . . It's enormous with a wall-to-wall swimming pool and a butler behind each life preserver. . . .

Last night a producer named Carlton Alsop took us to Romanoff's for a divine dinner, then we went to Joe Mankiewicz's house, met Herbert Marshall, very nice and very English. . . . Sunday we went to Malibu Beach to Irwin Shaw's house where he is deep at work on the scenario of his novel, *Arch of Triumph*. . . .

Saturday night was a real Hollywood party, which Harry Kurnitz gave for the Ira Gershwins. Harry is a writer, and every good writer in Hollywood was there—about a hundred people in all, and all for dinner . . . an enormous buffet with bowls of caviar for centerpieces, and champagne in the finger bowls. They had some strolling gypsy violinists for entertainment, and Harry, who fancies himself a violinist, insisted on strolling and playing with them, which prompted Groucho Marx to say, "Kurnitz is setting Romania back twenty years. . . ."

GUESS who was my dinner partner last night? Hollywood's newest dreamboat, known as Sexy Rexy Harrison! He's here with his wife, a very cute biscuit named Lili Palmer. [I wouldn't *dream* of so frivolous a description of Miss Palmer today, for this beautiful, gifted actress has also joined the ranks of first-rate writers.] [Just the same, she *was* a very cute biscuit!]

I went to a little jamboree last night at Nunnally Johnson's, where they had ten cops to park the cars, frisk the customers and hold up the drunks. They built a tent that was attached to the house for the party, and anyone who could spell martini was there—five hundred strong. Can you imagine vintage champagne for that mob? By twelve o'clock those bums didn't know what they were drinking anyway. Believe it or not, Norma Shearer was still the most glorious thing around, so much more divine than the pseudo glamour girls with their dresses plunging to their pelvic bones, who were sidling up to Louis B. Mayer hoping that contact meant contract. The food was ambrosia, and it was one helluva clambake, my dears. I had a glorious time and gained five pounds. . . .

In re-reading some of those letters, it occurs to me that there were some people who were comparatively new in my life, who became and remained intimate friends. Martin had known them, usually, but I had not. Harry Kurnitz for instance—a prime example of what Martin calls a "life enhancer." Harry and Martin's friendship stemmed from when they were boys in Philadelphia, and I'd heard tales of the brilliant, pungent epigrams that flowed endlessly from Kurnitz's lips. I don't know what I'd pictured as the housing for these sallies—surely not this heavy-lidded, sand-colored, scraggly beanpole of a man who mumbled rather than spoke, so that you had to edge up very close to hear the nimble verbal play. Once you did, it was worth it—but in addition to that aspect of his personality, Harry had something more important. He was gentle and kind, a lousy violinist and a sucker for a soft touch. He never depended on malice for his humor, and—rare among wits—he was a terrific audience, capable of making you feel as though you were the most intelligent person he'd ever met.

I loved Harry—as I did and still do another of Martin's friends, Irwin Shaw, who became my friend too. Irwin is another who doesn't look at all like what he is, one of America's most gifted writers. Full of explosive laughter, and ready wit, he looks like a football-player *manqué*, ruddy-faced, bear-like, as though he'd be a lot more at home running down the field with a pigskin under his arm than sweating over a typewriter, turning out short stories, novels, scenarios and plays, in a prolific stream of superior quality.

No, judging from those girlish, unsophisticated letters, I

certainly didn't have much to complain about, not on the social side. And now that I was pregnant, I couldn't very well have worked in pictures even if anyone had wanted me. However, there was no reason for me not to work in radio, and a job did turn up. My agent wrote me that I was wanted to star in a new series, which would originate in California—the one I mentioned earlier, "The Adventures of Anne Scotland" (the private eyelash thing), so I was happily back at the microphone. My burgeoning belly didn't matter at all, since I had to convey everything with my voice. So what if I had to waddle into and out of the studio? What if I had to stand sideways at the microphone? I was back in action and delighted about it.

We had to give up Glenda's house in the Valley, so we moved into a compound of villas called the Garden of Allah which, in addition to being more convenient and having a swimming pool, was the home of several of our friends. If need be, we could borrow a cup of scotch from Bob Benchley or Tallulah Bankhead, who always kept some on the premises (for medicinal purposes, of course), or we could borrow a cup of jokes from the Arthur Kobers or swap some nostalgic New York talk with Humphrey Bogart and Lauren Bacall. All in all it was a merry place to be, and it had an advantage which was important to *me*. Unlike most residences in the west Los Angeles area, we could actually walk to several places. I don't like car-living, seeing the world through a windshield, but everyone who prefers walking in that neck of the woods is regarded as some kind of nut, and it has become a cliché that the police of Beverly Hills cruise around and stop and question people who are merely out for a stroll. (It's a cliché because it is true, which is often the case with clichés.)

Thus it was terribly nice to be able to run across the road to a restaurant called The Players, which was owned by (of all people) one of the most gifted talents in the motion picture world, Preston Sturgis. (Like many another creative person, this brilliant author-director felt it necessary to have a little business on the side as a hedge against the day his creativity might run out. His life ran out before that happened, a great blow to the picture industry.) At any rate, The Players was literally across the road, but Bob Benchley used to send for a car to take him there. He said that the reason he didn't walk there was because he didn't want Southern Californians to think he was eccentric.

■

Martin's picture, *Smash-Up,* was progressing nicely, and it began to seem as though we would be in California for a longer period than I had bargained for. On the strength of the enthusiasm generated by how well Martin was doing, he was getting other offers to produce and direct pictures, and he had already agreed to direct an adaptation of the Henry James novel *The Aspern Papers.*

These developments produced mixed emotions in me, to say the least, for while I was proud and happy for Martin that he was having such success, I could not even entertain the idea of staying out there on a permanent basis. Theatrical success is ephemeral, and I was desperately afraid that if I stayed away too long, the erosion of my career, which I felt had already begun to set in, would accelerate and become irreversible.

That, by the way, is not as paranoid as it might sound. "Out of sight, out of mind" applies with even greater force to entertainers than to lovers, and I didn't want to be out of sight too long. Still, as there was not much I could do about it until after the baby was born, I made a very determined effort not to worry about what *might* happen, but rather just to relax and enjoy what *was* happening. I recorded all that faithfully in the pink-ribbon-tied bundle of letters to my parents, which contained descriptions of the elevated company of which I was a part, told how Ronald Colman worshipped the ground I walked on, how Greer Garson had told Martin that his VE-day broadcast had been one of the most memorable performances of our time, and other highly exaggerated bits of parent-cheering fluff.

Of all the parties we attended, the dinner I remember best was the one on January 28, 1947, at The Players, where Martin and I had taken our guest, Aldous Huxley.

Mr. Huxley at that time was a great enthusiast of yoga, and he regaled us during dinner with tales of the miraculous results he had achieved with the eye exercises. "You may remember," he said, "that I used to wear those thick eyeglasses?" We remembered. "Well," he continued, "I no longer need them, thanks to yoga." With that he picked up the menu to read, and bumped himself in the nose as he tried to bring it up to eye level.

I repressed my desire to laugh with such force that I'm

sure it was that which brought on my labor pains. The baby wasn't due, but as he had no calendar, he probably interpreted that spasm of inward hysteria as a signal. He's always hated to miss a joke.

"Martin," I said as calmly as I could, "I think I have to go back to the Garden of Allah," and from that moment on it was a Keystone Komedy sequence.

There is no way to say it elegantly: the water broke, and we scurried all around the Garden of Allah, gathering up spare turkish towels and wrapping me up in them. Martin got out our second-hand LaSalle touring car to drive me to the hospital. He is not Barney Oldfield under the best of circumstances, and so it was a ride I am not likely to forget. At fifteen miles an hour, nervous as a cat, he weaved from one side of the road to the other while I let out piercing shrieks of pain alternating with terror: *"Care*ful, *look* where you're *going! Oh oooooh OH!"*

We barely made it, Martin into oblivion and I into the delivery room, before Peter arrived. Suddenly the world was perfect.

I, of course, was glad to have a baby with all the working parts in order, but Martin! Martin was not to be contained for the joy of having a son!!! He went out and woke up a florist and had him send me three dozen Talisman roses, and I must remember to ask him some day who he managed to get to drive him home that night. I'm absolutely certain he couldn't have managed it himself.

8

We asked Lou Calhern to be Peter's godfather, not so much because we expected him to do what godfathers are supposed to do—that is, furnish religious guidance—but because he seemed the ideal person to teach Peter how to hold a bottle. That, at least, was the reason we gave him when we broached the subject, because in those days sentimental was not the "in" thing to be.

Actually we were *very* sentimental in our feelings about Lou. He had what Cole Porter once referred to in a song as "Klass with a capital 'K'" and Martin and I were deeply devoted to him. He was urbane, witty, and his good manners were the kind which can't be learned, because they came from inside, from an instinctual and genuine consideration for the people around him. Feeling as we did about him, and because Lou was long on kith but short on kin (unless you counted four ex-wives), we wanted to give him a rooting interest in a son, and to weld him even more closely into our family than he already was.

He accepted with pleasure, and when, shortly after Peter was born, Lou and Marianne had to go back to New York for a play, he struck up a correspondence with our two-month-old son, which I used to read to him as he lay in his crib, kicking, spitting, cooing and gurgling.

"Dear Peter," a typical letter would read,

James Cannon is going with one of the Dowling girls. Not the one who once went with Gadget Kazan, but the other one.

Sardi's has a new kitchen made of stainless steel and there's a machine for washing glasses there that does away with drying them altogether because the water is 300 degrees hot and it evaporates the minute the glass comes out.

They are digging up Madison Avenue something fierce at 57th Street.

Billingsley [owner of the famed Stork Club] presented me with a tie in which I would not be seen dead and I am forwarding it to your father because he resides in a clime where such neckwear goes unnoticed and if he doesn't like it will he please give it to the boy in the parking lot who dusts the cars and oblige two of us?

Bert Lahr is a serious proposition and no clown since his dramatic success [in *Waiting for Godot*] and he bemoans the paucity of playwrights.

Business is off, you little delinquent.

Incidentally, if anyone thinks I exaggerated that incident of my lugging crates and suitcases into the house, herewith the proof—an excerpt from a letter which I thought of having framed.

I emulate your father. I have seen him where there has been household activity and it's touching how calmly he takes it. I saw your mother furnish a whole house over his head and he didn't even notice it, and Peter, I want you to grow up like that. I think he'd have envied me today if he could have seen me draw my feet under me as Slats [his nickname for Marianne, because she didn't look like the kind of person anyone would dream of calling Slats] passed by with a trunk in her arms and it's a good ninety in the shade here. Trunk was full, too. I may have more actual calendar experience than your old dad, but son, he's a real husband and I'm willing to sit at his feet and learn. He would have looked at that trunk and said, "What's that?" but I don't think of things like that until too late so I just gathered my feet out of the way and kept my mouth shut like a dolt. . .

Peter says that Lou's letters evoke for him more about those days and about us than a time capsule could have done, and I agree that's true, but the part that touches me was that it was obvious that the godfather-godson relationship meant something more to Lou than just an honorary status, or having to remember when Peter's birthday was so that he could send him a present.

I have a sneaking suspicion that Lou and Martin envisioned being the Destiny That Shaped Peter's Ends, molding him along their own lines as a member of an elitist group whose members talk what used to be called *man-talk*. That, of course, was before the time of great discovery, when it was learned that women hardly ever swooned at the mention of a Giant-Dodger game, Brand A versus Brand B shaving cream, or even racy stories. Most certainly Lou and Martin envisaged somebody to carry on the magnificent tradition of sartorial splendor, as witness this letter from Lou to my three-month-old son:

Another cravat is on its way to your father. It was something I couldn't resist as I browsed through the shops to see what the trades were offering for fall and winter.

Which reminds me that when next you catch your father's ear, it might be well to suggest to him that the fine loose carefree association with [Irwin] Shaw and [Peter] Viertel is all very well and it may have cultural benefits and it may not. But there is sartorial laxness about them boys and maybe it's catching.

Their hushed wives are a different matter. Ladies, ladies in the good old accepted sense who are seen and not heard and seem to move gracefully in full knowledge of their places. This I like to see and never do around my joint. Nor yours. Peter my boy, I love you and your family.

Lou.

How glad I am that we were able to let him share Peter with us, because I know it enriched his life as he had enriched ours, with his humor, his offbeat slant on man's condition, his surprising wisdom about people, and most of all, his incomparable gift of friendship. We miss him every day of our lives.

Before Peter was born, Martin went around telling everyone that we were going to name our son David Garrick Gabel. "Our *son*?" I screamed. "Who gave you an inside track on what we're going to have?"

"Don't be silly" was his reasonable reply.

When it developed that he'd guessed right about the sex, I started throwing up roadblocks about the name. "What will the kids in school say?" "How do you know he'll even *want* to be an actor?"

"Don't be silly" was his reasonable reply.

Though he would not abandon the idea of an actor-son, he made a concession to me on the name. However, from the moment of Peter's birth, instead of crooning "Rockabye Baby" as any civilian (non-theatrical) father would have done, he started brainwashing him by whispering in his ear, "All the world's a stage. . . ."

Without a lot of preparation, I was catapulted into the world of Pabulum and prams, and I was amazed at how much pleasure I could derive from the sound of a burp or the sight of a healthy b.m. For a while I even stopped thinking about working, but when it came over me that my physical presence every moment of the day and night was not actually required (thanks to a marvelous nurse whose double-talk Peter seemed to enjoy as much as he did mine), I started worrying again about my almost nonexistent career.

I would have taken anything that was offered at that point, except for Martin, who strongly advised me never to take just any old role, or a bit part in order to get started. "Not in pictures," he said. "It just doesn't work that way. If you establish yourself as a bit player, that's what you'll be. In this town, that's a fatal mistake. The only small roles you can play are cameos in prestige pictures." I knew he was right, but for me it was torture to sit around doing nothing.

The United States Marines in the form of Irving Reis and Chester Erskine came to the rescue with an offer to play a part in a picture which they were producing, the adaptation of Arthur Miller's play, *All My Sons*. This admirably filled Martin's specifications for the kind of job I should have. I would be acting in the company of Edward G. Robinson and Burt Lancaster, and who could ask for a more prestigious film than one with Arthur Miller's name on it? Indeed, I was so eager to do it that I didn't even raise a fuss about playing the entire part wearing a housedress!

While I was working it was marvelous—I enjoyed every minute of it, and what was more we came to be good friends with Edward G. Robinson, an exceptional bonus, for this cigar-chomping baddie of the gangster films turned out to be a *bon vivant* with a glorious sense of humor and an even more glorious collection of art. Knowing him added immeasurably to my pleasure in working in the film, but in all too short a time it was over, and I began to get that old feeling again, that itch to get back to "The Town," as Calhern called New York.

And this time a five-foot-two dynamo in the appealing form of Elisabeth Bergner came to my rescue. Miss Bergner had directed *The Overtons*, the play I'd done just before going to California, and now she was to star in a production about an alcoholic called *Cup of Trembling*, which her husband, Paul Czinner, would direct. She wanted me for the other female lead, that of a reformed alcoholic, and while I was terribly flattered and wanted with all my heart to play it, I had a few stabs of conscience about rushing off to New York, leaving a husband and an eight-month-old baby. Martin very generously urged me to take it, and he pointed out that Miss Peterson, our loving and competent nurse, could manage admirably where Peter was concerned.

A weaker protest you never heard. "Are you *sure*?" and "You honestly don't mind?" and a few blatant lies such as how it wasn't all that important to me, I could take it or leave it alone—and I rushed to my nearest telegraph office and sent off a wire of acceptance to Miss Bergner.

It was positively unseemly, the joy I felt at leaving California, and I hasten to add that it had nothing to do with California, only with me. We had met some attractive and gifted people, and though our closest friends were other New Yorkers-in-exile, as we felt ourselves to be, there were several new friends who were in the picture business, who were delightful people and who have become permanent additions to our lives.

It should be remembered that I am here talking about a Hollywood which practically is nonexistent now, so changed is the industry. At that time it was terribly parochial, as I'm sure almost anyone would admit. We were bound together almost exclusively by film and to that extent we were practically an incestuous community. Even without *Cup of Trembling* to draw me back, I longed for, missed terribly, the sights and sounds and smells and diverse stimuli of New York.

I had a strong hunch that Martin would be following me back to New York before too long, because I had noticed that he was paying greater attention to the plays that were sent to him, than to movie scenarios. And that was how it turned out, in just a few months—by which time I was so lonesome for both my men, I could hardly bear it.

When Martin called to tell me they were coming back to New York, *Cup of Trembling* was already playing, and I couldn't go out and close up the California house. That gave me a few uneasy moments, but it couldn't be helped, and this is my first opportunity to make a public apology to Martin for thinking that he wouldn't be able to manage the details. Despite Calhern's (and my) low opinion of my husband as a domestic animal, he managed to take care of everything and, what is more, to bring Peter in his arms all the way to New York. There are many among our friends who know Martin well and who will say I invented all this, but they will have to accept my word that it is true.

The reason it is all seared on my memory is because of the terror I felt standing in the airport, waiting for them to arrive. Would Peter be all in one piece? Would Martin have survived however many hours it took in those days to fly from California, of feeding, of dressing, of calming a nine-month-old baby? And suddenly there they came, Peter tooling along on his own two feet, an event which put me in shock because I'd never seen him walk before. What is more, he was gloriously attired in a blue snowsuit, with a diaper hanging out of one leg and trailing him like a plume. Martin looked smug and happy, and I was a laughing-crying wreck.

And so we were all three home again. Two of us were terribly happy about it, and the third one was mildly curious about his new environment. I think he missed Miss Peterson, his nurse, for a while—one is always sentimental about the first woman in one's life, and I was reasonably sure she *was* his paramour, judging by the cooing and gurgling that had gone on whenever she entered the room. (I remember believing her absolutely when she told me one day, looking at Peter's equipment as she changed his diaper, "That's a sure sign he'll have big feet!") Anyway, he got used to me after a while, and I think he got to like me too.

Cup of Trembling wasn't exactly a success—a few weeks in Boston (where people sometimes waited for me at the stage door, confusing me with my stage role as a reformed alcoholic, to ask how I had overcome *my* problem because they had this relative, who was also an alcoholic, etc., etc.)—and a few weeks in New York. It wasn't a *bad* play; it was just that it was such a downer, more a preachment than a dramatic event.

Still, it was thrilling to work on the same stage with Miss Bergner who, in addition to her enormous talent, had the greatest professional discipline I've ever seen. And the greatest show-wisdom, I guess you could call it. I remember one day during rehearsal, she said, as I was sitting in one place playing a scene alone with her, "Lissen, sveet vun, in dis scene you must go around from place to place, very nervous, in a continual movement, und *I* vill sit absolutely still in the center, lissening to you. *All eyes vill be vatching YOU!*" I was about as theater-wise as a rabbit, and I thought, "How generous!" Naturally everyone would watch Miss B., the eye of the hurricane. Just the same, I thought, I think she is one of the most superior actresses I have ever seen. I don't know what she thought of me as an actress, but it occurred to me at one point that she had a rather sophisticated interest in me as a person. The point I'm talking about was when we were posing for a picture together as her husband stood off in the sidelines watching. I beckoned to him. "Come on, Paul," I said, "Get in the picture! What good are two women without a man?" I meant it to be gay, but only in the old-fashioned sense of the word, and I almost fell over backward when Miss Bergner looked at me out of the corner of her eye and said, "Darrrlink, you dun't know?"

It was a time when we had troops everywhere in the world—occupying Germany, South Korea, Japan and so on—and it occurred to the producers of the radio success "Blind Date," that we still had enough men in uniform to put the show back on the air, but this time on TV.

It was a tremendous success right from the beginning, and I had my first acquaintance with what it was like to be recognized wherever I went. Here was a powerful new medium, and I was in at the start of it. We were debuting together, as it were. I'll not go into the sociological factors which such great power brings—I'm speaking only from the point of view of what it means to a performer. At that time, it was an absolute revelation, for none of us was used to it.

85

I'd had my picture in the paper hundreds of times, I'd done dozens of plays and radio shows, even a movie, but it had always been possible for me to go almost anywhere with only the stray theater-goer recognizing me in a public place. With television, that entire picture changed, and I got to be "Arlene" to all those people driving cabs or selling behind counters or running elevators. I had a whole family I had known nothing about, and they were dear, appreciative, and hardly ever nuisances!

And Martin was terrific about it all. If we walked down the street and someone asked for an autograph, he'd smile and walk on ahead, and if whoever it was said they wanted his as well, he'd say, "No, of course you don't, it's perfectly all right," or something equally gracious. He says if he ever writes an autobiography he'll call it *And You Too, Mr. Gabel!*

One of my favorite memories of that period was getting into a cab and having the driver say, "What's Marty doing now, Arlene?"

"He's playing in *King Lear,*" I said, "with Lou Calhern."

The driver, a grizzled man with a Jewish accent, seemed astonished. "*King Lear?*" he said. "Tell me, is that any good in English?"

I didn't quite understand what that was all about until Martin explained to me later that *King Lear,* because of its theme of the perfidy of children, has traditionally been a great tear-jerker in the Yiddish theater, and has been performed by all the most prominent Yiddish actors.

And *King Lear* is the source of another memory, this one concerning Peter. He was only about three years old, but I didn't care. I thought that as a member of our family he should see his father (to say nothing of his godfather) in a Shakespearean production. Martin was playing the Duke of Kent, and at one point, Lear flays him with words, banishing him from the kingdom. Peter had been sitting as quietly as an angel up to that point, but I felt his little body tense up and finally, unable to contain himself any longer, he piped out, "Uncle Lou shouldn't talk to Daddy like that!" He broke up the entire audience, and the cast had a hard time keeping its composure too. I had to drag him out of the theater.

Speaking of Peter, for a while there it seemed to me that Martin was right, that he *was* going to be an actor. He started

exhibiting a few traits, not necessarily of talent, but of temper-
ament. I took him to Billy Reed's Little Club for the annual
Christmas party for the children of people in the theater. A
highlight of the party was a coast-to-coast broadcast, with all
the tykes doing whatever clever things their parents had
forced them to learn for the occasion.

As I have related, Marty's contribution to Peter's education had been bludgeoning him from infancy to learn the
"Seven Ages of Man" soliloquy from *As You Like It,* and now
he sat on my lap, staring at the microphone which had been
placed before him. I nudged him to begin and he did. . . .

" 'All the world's a stage . . .' What's this, Mommy?"

"Shhh dear, that's called a microphone. Go *on* . . . 'All the
world's a stage and . . .' "

" 'And all the men and women merely players . . .' What's
it for?"

"Your voice goes into it. *Please* Peter, go *on* darling."

" 'They have their exits and their entrances . . .'
Whadaya mean, my voice goes into it? Where does it come
out?"

"In people's houses."

"*Mom*my!" [You liar.] "You're *sure*?"

And so on. By the time he got to the seventh age of man,
I was practically at that point myself. Peter was a wild success,
however, with mail and phone calls and most people convinced that it was a comedy routine we had worked out.

Just the same, Martin's efforts to make an actor of Peter
went for nothing. We reached that conclusion some years later
when we did a *Person to Person* broadcast with Ed Murrow.
That show consisted of interviews with people who were
known to the public for one reason or another, in their own
homes. Ed spoke to them from the studio by remote control,
as though he were actually in their home. It's a commonplace
technique now, but at that time it was brand new, and the
show was very successful because it was based on our good old
American nosiness about what goes on in other peoples'
houses.

But about Peter, we wanted him to be part of the interview, and he agreed with, it seemed to me, pleasure. He even
suggested that he might play the violin, which he was study-
ing. Martin said, "What about 'America'?" and he said, "Sure,

why not?" (This was, remember, the McCarthy era, and "America" seemed a felicitous choice. Nobody was going to blacklist *our* six-year-old!) Peter played it with all the assurance of a young Heifetz, but unfortunately without much of his talent. As a matter of fact, his rendition was so awful, it *could* have been considered subversive.

Mr. Murrow applauded generously when he had finished, and said, "Do you have any idea about following in your parents' footsteps?"

"No, I don't think so," Peter replied thoughtfully. "I'm not sure what I want to be. A baseball player maybe." What a relief this must have been to all the violin prodigies who may have been listening! The point, however, is that Peter was as forthright then as he is now, and that he was not in the least intimidated by his surroundings, or by the importance of the great Ed Murrow. Even then he was in rehearsal for making his own decisions. (And while ours might have been different, on occasion, from those which he made, we are terribly proud of the development of his character which has made him always his own person.)

A number of the comic occurrences on various television shows in which I had a part, didn't seem all that comic when they were happening. I'm speaking of unrehearsed things. It's one thing if you're prepared for a pie in your face, but I don't see how you could ever be prepared for having a monkey fall madly in love with you at sight!

That happened on "Blind Date." How it happened or who brought him I don't recall, but there was a monkey, and his name was Bonzo, and he took one look at me and *zing went the strings of his heart.* He had his arms around my neck before you could say Buck Rogers, carried on, climbed all over me, chattering little love noises that had me and the audience laughing so hard we couldn't get on with the show. "All right now, Bonz," I said, "that's enough. Down boy. See you later." He paid no attention.

I adopted a sterner tone, one that would brook no nonsense. "You have to go now. That is a-l-l, all. Goodbye, *do you hear me?"*

Something in my tone must have gotten to him, because he became very angry with me. Hell, obviously, hath no fury like a monkey scorned, and he leaned over and deliberately bit my finger. The keeper rushed out of the wings and clubbed him lightly on the head so that he would let go, and then dragged him away. My finger was bleeding copiously but, not wishing to disrupt the show, I just wrapped it in the folds of my evening dress and carried on until the final commercial. The minute we were off the air, the producer came rushing out and asked if there was a doctor in the house. Fortunately there was one, and he hustled on stage, bandaged my finger, and then rushed me downstairs into a waiting car and over to the emergency room of a hospital so that I could get a tetanus shot.

I was perfectly fine, but the next day the monkey died. I don't think it took ten minutes for this news to circulate through NBC, CBS, ABC, channels 4, 2, 7, 5, 9, 11 and 13, if they were all in existence at that time—"Dja hear about the monkey who bit Arlene? He died. They gave the wrong one the tetanus shot, yuk yuk," and other witty remarks. (Just to clear my good name, and for the record, a fire broke out where they had caged the poor monkey, and he died of smoke inhalation, but I'll never convince anyone who was around the studios in those days of that.)

Viewer or doer, one way or another television affected peoples' lives. I don't believe the degree to which almost everyone is influenced by what he or she sees on this colossus has been fully realized even now, and I will leave value judgments to people in the value judgment business. Speaking strictly for myself, TV changed the entire thrust of my career, and it also affected me in other, subtler ways where my public behavior was concerned.

As an actress, what counted was my performance in the role I was playing. Certainly there was a passing interest in my private life as there is with all performers (*something* must account for the sale of all those fan magazines!), but nothing noteworthy. With the advent of big-time television and my own emergence as a "personality," that changed. Suddenly I found that I was careful of what I might say or do in public, wary of expressing personal opinions which might embarrass a sponsor or the network, rather protective of something called "my image." We who work in this industry have, over the past several years, become less diffident about expressing ourselves, I believe, but one does develop a pattern of behavior, and that is difficult to change.

DON'T ANTAGONIZE!
DON'T MAKE WAVES!
IF YOU WIN, ACT AS THOUGH YOU'RE USED TO IT!
IF YOU LOSE, ACT AS THOUGH YOU LIKE IT!

That was my credo pretty much, but I didn't have to tack it up on my mirror. I needed no reminding that what I said, how I looked, what I wore and where I went would be noted and probably recorded, and my public personality was shaped around that knowledge. My own need for approval, aided and abetted by the policy of the industry in which I worked—that of never taking a stand which might be considered "controversial"—succeeded in firming up a mold which I still find very difficult to break out of. Even among friends, I often have to rev myself up inwardly before I have enough steam to voice an opinion in contradiction to what is being said.

This public image thing began with "Blind Date," continued through "Soldier Parade," "Talent Patrol" and a few others, but it really got to be a major factor in my life after a phone call one day in 1950 from a dedicated entrepreneur named Mark Goodson. There was nothing spectacular about the call—it was the sort of thing that happened quite often: a work proposition.

"Arlene," he said, "would you try out an idea with us? It's for a summer replacement, just a thirteen-week deal, but we have John Daly and Dorothy Kilgallen coming over to the house Sunday to see if it works, and we need you. So it won't be a total loss, I'll give you tea and crumpets."

I asked what kind of show, and he said it was a game show, and that this one was really different. "How different?" I wanted to know.

"Well, nobody gets big prizes, there are no funny gag writers, no gimmicky tricks, nothing."

"That's *good?*"

"We think so. It's based on a simple proposition that Americans have a habit of following up on 'How do you do?'

when they've been introduced with '*What* do you do?' We're going to call it 'What's My Line?' Interested?"

It didn't sound wildly exciting, which is why Goodson-Todman are millionaire producers and I'm not, but I told him to put the kettle on, that I'd be there.

As everyone probably knows, the little thirteen-week deal ran for a quarter of a century, and I ran right along with it. It changed my life on a number of levels, and forced me into one of those irrevocable choices I have had to make in my life—this one having to do with my career. It was utterly impossible for me, from that moment on, to regard the theater as my major aim, for I could never be too far from where "What's My Line?" was broadcasting. As if to compensate for depriving me of something I loved, my constant exposure on the show put me in rather flattering demand for other shows. That's the way those things work. Everybody wants you when somebody else has you (in life, too, I think) and I was offered as much work as I was physically capable of handling.

"What's My Line?" was upbeat, unpredictable, challenging, and some of the greatest fun I've ever had—in or out of a job. It turned out to be not so much a show for me and for the others involved in it, but a way of life.

9

I've always told everyone I was on "What's My Line?" from the very beginning, and unless you want to quibble about it, that's true. If you *do* want to, the fact is that I missed the first show, and my place was taken by ex-Governor Hoffman of New Jersey. I don't honestly remember why I missed it, but I think I had committed myself to something else, some other program that night, and I suppose I made no great effort to get out of it because, as I have indicated, I didn't think anything earth-shaking was going to result from this modest little show which we'd tried out in Mark Goodson's apartment.

As he had truthfully stated, there were no gimmicks or huge sums of money involved. Just think about other game shows, and you'll see what I mean. "You've just won a trip to the moon on gossamer wings," says the manic M.C., "and your own private C-130, which is going to fly you to Egypt to float down the Nile on Cleopatra's barge, which comes fully equipped with this fantastic Wurlitzer Organ and Westing-house Kitchen!" The overweight housewife who knew who was buried in Grant's Tomb faints from sheer ecstasy and the studio audience goes mad. On the other hand, "What's My Line?" dispensed a maximum of fifty dollars to each contestant and never raised the price a quarter in twenty-five years.

There were no joke writers or world-famous personalities involved on the panel; in fact there was nothing to make a really big splurge from a publicity point of view, and we weren't going to be on prime time or anything like that. When we started in February, 1950, we were on every other Tuesday, and in the summer we replaced a show which had been playing on Sundays. We figured we'd be lucky to pick up the few stragglers who had nothing better to do on Tuesday nights when it was too cold to go out to bowl, and though we knew we had a *few* modest attainments as a show, at best we thought of ourselves as a pleasant little diversion.

Now, of course, Mark and Bill claim they knew all along they had a tiger by the tail, but I think nobody really expected us to have the impact we had. The initial response was positively staggering, for we had apparently struck gold. We had touched (as indeed Mark had said we would) on that irrepressible desire to know what our neighbors do for a living. (I'm told by Europeans that this is a peculiarly American characteristic, that we are the *only* ones actually—eckshully, that is—who ask such personal questions of people we've just met.)

With the exception of that first show, the original panel had, in addition to me, Dorothy Kilgallen, a psychiatrist named Dr. Hoffman, and Louis Untermeyer, poet and anthologist. In a few weeks the psychiatrist was replaced by a comedy writer named Hal Block, and six months or so later, Louis Untermeyer was replaced by Bennett Cerf, under circumstances which we were all pretty ashamed of, but which we could do nothing about. (These were the days of the intimidation of networks and sponsors by Senator Joseph McCarthy and by the House Committee on Un-American Activities, and Louis was suspected of having friends on the left side of the political spectrum. It is hard to credit that such a *suspicion* was enough to deprive a man of his right to work. And in this country! Nevertheless it was so, and nobody felt strong enough to fight the tide of reaction which had overtaken the country. Rather than make an issue of it, a replacement was quietly found. I must admit Bennett was a glorious replacement.)

The Hal Block spot was vacated after a while and a number of others filled it at varying times, the most notable being Fred Allen, who stayed with it until his death. Eventually we got another great Allen—Steve, whose famous contribution to the show was the phrase which became part of the American language—"Is it bigger than a breadbox?" It was born while he was trying to guess a product our contestant sold.

Between the two Allens there was a long parade of people who, for one reason or another, simply weren't right. It isn't that they weren't funny or that they couldn't talk or play the game, it was just that they didn't mix well with the rest of us. Putting that panel together was a bit like a recipe for a cake. The ingredients had to be in the right proportion, or the cake wouldn't rise.

The mix that worked for *us* was:

One (1) slightly acerbic wit, a tiny bit wicked but tremendously bright. Dorothy Kilgallen.

One (1) basically good girl who sometimes said marginally sexy things (Example: To a terribly attractive contestant, "I don't know what you do, but whatever it is, I'd like to do it with you.") Guess who?

One (1) Peck's Bad Boy. Fred Allen, Steve Allen, et al.

One (1) urbane wit, sort of intellectual, but not dangerously so. Bennett Cerf.

One (1) sophisticated, but not condescending, knowledgeable pundit. John Daly.

Dressing in evening clothes gave our show a look of casual elegance, and we tried to convey the impression that we *always* dressed that way after dark. When the "walk-in" entrance was canceled to save more time for the playing of the game, people called in irritation because they wanted the fashion show! It actually was more like a visit than a theatrical presentation, largely because the ad-libs were genuine, and of course, unpredictable.

I think that ad-lib quality was one of the show's greatest assets. The tension and excitement were terrific for all of us, because in the 50s everything was "live," which meant that if you made a mistake you couldn't take it back, couldn't erase it as you can erase tape, and that very sense of immediacy communicated itself to the audience. There's something to be said for imperfection—it's more human. For the first seven years, "What's My Line?" was broadcast as it was performed—live before an audience—and because of the whole spontaneous quality of the show, I think those were the best years.

Even the clinkers which happened *because* we were live turned out to have a plus value; if we'd been on tape, how could we have had as one of our early guests an attractive young woman who had given her occupation as a plumber's assistant? Goodson-Todman's security checking system hadn't been perfected as yet I suppose, and so it developed that our contestant might very well have assisted a plumber here and there, but goodness only knows at what, since her profession was a prostitute. Now *that*, I think, was very enterprising on her part—getting herself all that free advertising on national TV and follow-up coverage in the press! The show hadn't been on five minutes with this female before the switchboard lit up, besieged by some viewers who had apparently had plumbing problems in the past that had been attended to by our contestant and who couldn't wait to let us know.

And if we'd been taped, I doubt our audience would have ever seen the contestant who said he washed elephants for a living, but who, it developed, was a car thief from Detroit. It just so happened that an astute Detroit policeman, a fan of the show with a good memory, was watching; he wired the New York Police Department, who sent a committee to greet our contestant when he came out of the studio. I cannot imagine what he could have been thinking of when he asked to be on the show. That we were just a local program, seen in New York only? I guess I'll never know.

We also had a bit of a flap one time when Milton Berle was the mystery guest. Somebody from the audience—obviously a nut—jumped up on the stage and started shouting "Happy Mother's Day!" Fortunately he was harmless, but it gave us a turn to realize how vulnerable we all were, up there like sitting ducks for somebody who might *not* be so harmless.

Tape, too, would have eliminated other types of cliffhangers, some of them having to do with the regular feature, the Mystery Guest. The most traumatic in the memories of the producers was something about which the panelists knew nothing, obviously, since we never knew who the mystery guest would be. This had to do with the appearance of Judy Garland, who was noted for a lot of things that were wonderful, but reliability was not one of them.

In charge of getting mystery guests for the show was Bob Bach, a music buff who numbered (and numbers) among his friends most of the great jazz singers and musicians. He persuaded Judy that it would be good for her career (which was at that time in a bit of a slump) if she were to appear on "What's My Line?" and he assured Goodson and Todman that she would behave professionally, i.e., be on time, be sober and be *there*. When she was forty minutes late in arriving, even Bob was biting his nails, and Mark was pacing the floor, I am told. She arrived twenty minutes before she was due to go on, and Bob hustled her to her dressing room and left her there. Ten minutes went by, and Mark sent someone to see how she was doing. The young woman came rushing back in tears to report to Mark that Judy had told her to get the hell out and stay out!

Bob said to Mark, "You shouldn't have sent anyone but me. It's my responsibility to see that she gets on, and I'll do it. Judy isn't a child, she's a star!" But he ate his words five minutes later when she still hadn't appeared, and he went back himself to check on her. "Jesus," he said, coming out of her dressing room, "her hair is still in curlers."

Mark sent a note out to John Daly immediately, saying, "Forget about Garland. I'm the mystery guest," and started straightening his tie. He picked up the chalk just as John began his familiar routine: "And now it's time for the regular feature . . ." and at exactly that point Judy came out of her dressing room.

"How much time do I have?" she asked.

"Five seconds," Mark replied.

"Well then," she said taking the chalk out of his hand, "what the fuck was the rush?" and out she strode to deafening applause. Like the man had said, she was a star.

On another night, two mystery guests showed up—Errol Flynn and Lloyd Nolan, both demanding to go on, both insisting that it would be impossible for either of them to come back. It had been the producer's impression that Errol had said he couldn't go on because he had a heavy date in South America, but his story now was that he had postponed his date on our account. Several knee-bendings later, he agreed to come back the following week, and nobody ever learned what happened to the lady in South America—but as I say, if we'd been on tape we simply would have taped both shows and shown them whenever the producers decided to. It might not have been so much fun, but it would have produced fewer gray hairs on Mark's handsome head.

The Mystery Guest feature was the highlight of the show, even though it was a shameless plug for a movie, a book, a show, a cause of some kind or other. Nobody cared about that. They only cared about seeing these terribly famous people let their hair down, and these terribly famous people were delighted to oblige. They would grunt or groan or whisper or do whatever they thought would fool the panel for the chance to promote what they had come to promote.

I don't mean this in a pejorative sense at all. Wanting to sell something wasn't necessarily self-serving. The illustrious Eleanor Roosevelt, for example, came on "What's My Line?" to draw attention to a worthy cause in which she was interested, as did many others to speak on behalf of a charity or an educational project for which they hoped to draw support.

Stars of the status of Elizabeth Taylor, Roz Russell, Jack Benny, Jimmy Stewart, Joan Crawford, Bette Davis and all the rest probably were cooperating with their studios on the promotion of a current picture. Frank Sinatra came on, as did the great Satchmo himself, Louis Armstrong, and politicians by the dozen—Ronald Reagan (not yet Governor Reagan, but thinking ahead), golden-voiced Senator Everett Dirksen of Illinois (to whom I said from behind my blindfold, "I don't care *who* you are, I'm crazy about you! I'm susceptible to voices—me and Joan of Arc!"). And there was a handsome young hero named John Lindsay, at that time the representative in Congress of the Silk Stocking district of Manhattan, and governors of many states—the list goes on and on.

For whatever reasons they came on, most of our guests furnished the audience with gales of laughter once they were there. Jack Benny, for instance, signing himself in as Jascha Heifetz; Satchmo singing us a chorus of "Hello Dolly" at my request, after we had guessed him; the incomparable Bea Lillie doing a comic turn at Bennett's request—a host of fleeting, golden moments of fun. And the panelists themselves, guest panelists, could always be counted on to contribute to the gaiety. As when the blindfolded Dick Cavett, noting the applause accorded our mystery guest, Gina Lollobrigida, opened by saying, "Gee, you're either very popular or nude." And a little exchange I remember between Fred Allen and a guest:

Allen: "Sir, this is your first appearance on this show, is it not?"

Guest: "Yes, it is."

Allen: "And this is my first appearance on the show too, so in that case you and I could save a lot of time if you'll just tell me what you do for a living."

We all contributed to break-ups at one time or other. Even I, when Gene Tierney was our mystery guest and Dorothy Kilgallen asked if she needed any special equipment for her job. She said no, she didn't, and John Daly, as he often did, said, "Small conference." We waited while he whispered to her, and I said, "He's investigating her equipment."

Time and again I was asked, "C'mon now, don't you ever get any advance information about who the mystery guest will be?" and the answer was always honestly *no*. We did try to figure it out on our own—reading the paper to see who was in town, that sort of thing—and there were a few occasions when somebody spilled the beans to someone on the panel, but it was a point of honor with all of us to disqualify ourselves when that happened. But it wasn't coming up with the right answers that counted. Who cared, after all, whether you guessed correctly or not? The fun was in the inventiveness of the questions and the improvisational quality of the humor, which made for the success of the show. The real moments of embarrassment that I remember were *not* guessing somebody who really *wanted* to be guessed, because such is the nature of man (particularly a performer) that he would like to think of himself as so unique that he could not fail to be recognized, even under a disguised voice. I noticed over the years that our mystery guests were always much happier to be guessed than to have fooled the panelists.

"What's My Line?" proved to be such a success that a British version went on BBC, and I exchanged places as a guest with a member of their panel named Barbara Kelly. One English contribution to the show was the hospitality room, where we all gathered before going on stage. Here a bar was set up and short of hiccoughs, you could have anything you wanted. In America, on the other hand, you practically had to take a breatholater test before they let you go on stage! Another contribution was in the format of the show itself—the English allowed for mime in the identification of occupations. I thought that would be a dead giveaway, and when one of the contestants mimed that he was holding something in one hand and slathering back and forth over it with the other, I thought it was perfectly clear that he sold hot dogs. Not at all. He was a lipstick polisher. (I suppose somebody polishes lipstick, but I'd never given it a thought.)

I don't think I covered myself with glory as a guesser, but I had a lot of fun. After all, I'd never *heard* of a flint knapper, which was the occupation of one of the English contestants. I'd always thought that flints were something you rubbed two boy scouts together with to make a fire, but it turned out that a flint knapper is someone who chops down flints to fit into blunderbusses, which are sent to South Africa. Don't look at *me*. I didn't make it up, and besides, maybe they don't send blunderbusses to South Africa any more. As for the English Mystery Guest, I wouldn't even have required a blindfold, though of course everyone wore one. Well, would *you* have guessed Sir Don Bradman, Australia's top cricket batsman? Not bloody likely! Not for someone who had never found cricket exactly riveting. However, I *did* get Sir Gordon Richards, the jockey who rode *Pinza,* the Derby winner. I had bet on him during Coronation Week.

Over the years we were able to bring to the American public informal glimpses of the most famous people in America and from other parts of the world as well. Our mystery guests are a Hall of Fame roster and, as I have said, they all had something they wanted to bring to the attention of the American people. But it was quid pro quo: we allowed them to publicize whatever it was, and they, by their appearance, kept our ratings way up there.

In playing the game, I think all of us—the panelists, that is—sharply developed our intuitive sense. That happens when you play a game long enough. I certainly had no radar, but we had, for example, a feature called "The Wild Guess" for a while, where John Daly asked each panelist in turn, before the questioning had started, to guess the contestant's occupation. A mild-mannered youngish man appeared one night, and I asked, "Are you an atomic scientist?" When he said "yes," I almost fainted.

But the "radar" was far from reliable. The mystery guest one night was my son Peter, and I missed him completely, even when somebody asked him if he worked at the World's Fair, where Peter had a job that summer. He said yes, he did, and I *still* had no idea who it was. The audience always loved it when we failed with someone we ought to know. Dorothy, for instance, missed on a customs officer who had given her a very

26

27

28

29

26. Me, Bennett Cerf, Dorothy Kilgallen and John Daly—"What's My Line?" (as if you didn't know).
27 Same quartet, same show (as if you didn't know).
28. Woman of the Year.
29. With Robert Forster in *Mrs. Dally* (wearing the wig that saved my skull).
30. Martin. Could he be worried about the billing?

30

hard time just a few days earlier, making her unpack every item of luggage. And I missed a police officer who had given me a ticket the day before . . . and we weren't wearing masks. When Jayne Meadows was on, it was Bennett who identified her, not Steve Allen, her husband.

Among the panelists, the interpersonal relationships were very pleasant, in varying degrees. The Cerfs became our close, intimate friends—we even bought a few acres of Bennett's property in Mount Kisco and built our own house on it, so that we were not only colleagues, but neighbors, at least on weekends.

As for Dorothy Kilgallen and her husband, Richard Kollmar, we were not on that same level of intimacy, but I yield to nobody in my admiration for her sharp, penetrating mind. Dorothy and I were philosophically in different camps, she a conservative Republican with a column which ran in the Hearst papers, and I a liberal Democrat. This would certainly not be a cause for hostility—nor was it—except that the show started in 1950, and as I have said, Senator McCarthy and the House Committee on Un-American Activities were riding high. I was extremely sensitive to the criticisms leveled at many of my friends who were dubbed "leftish" when it suited their critics, and I felt that Dorothy sometimes used her column to attack people with whose politics she disagreed. However, between the two of *us*, there was never a cross word, and I believe she had as much respect for me as I did for her. Once a year we went to her house for the tree-lighting ceremony on Christmas Eve, and she came to our house for people-lighting whenever there was an excuse for it.

After the Sunday night show, we followed a sort of routine. Usually we went to supper with the Cerfs, to the Oak Room at the Plaza or Billy Reed's Little Club or the Stork— while Dorothy and Dick went off to P. J. Clarke's or the Peppermint Lounge (she was a sensational Twister) with Bob Bach and his wife Jean (who is now my producer at WOR). Sometimes the Goodsons came with us, sometimes they went with the Kollmars, maintaining an even balance, no doubt. Nothing was planned. It just worked out that way. John Daly, by the way, went alone to Toots Shor's to talk sports with Bob Considine and to rub shoulders with athletes. Like omnia Gallia, the panel in tres partes was divisum, but only socially. Professionally we were all for one and one for all.

I suppose it seemed to most of us that "What's My Line?," which had practically become an American institution, would go on forever, and in that form. It saddened us all to realize that it couldn't, and when it went off the air for a while, before it became a syndicated program aimed more towards the young, as so many other programs are these days, we understood that an important aspect of our lives had disappeared.

Of us all, I think Bennett was the most personally affected by the show. Most of us had had some direct or indirect connection with show business—Dorothy's husband, Richard Kollmar, was an actor and producer, so she was very theater oriented. Steve Allen, I don't have to say, is a performer. But Bennett was part of the book world, a dignified publisher of important books. We-e-ll, *dignified* may be an overstatement. He was actually quite mischievously funny, and one of the most atrocious punsters who ever walked the earth, but he certainly *had* dignity. Well-known in literary circles, he was nonetheless not at all prepared for the recognition which comes as a result of exposure on the tube. He found himself signing autographs, being asked to lecture all over the country, being pointed out in restaurants on the street, getting the low-bow treatment from headwaiters, and the rest of the fringe benefits which go with being a celebrity.

And he loved it! He told me he felt that one of the most engrossing, satisfying periods of his life had come to an end when the show went off as a national Sunday night pastime. Bennett was probably the only one among us who was completely happy being who he was—Bennett Cerf. I wanted to be a great actress; Dorothy Kilgallen wanted to be, well, perhaps Marilyn Monroe instead of the excellent newspaper woman she was; John Daly, the best of all moderators, wanted to be a newsman; and Steve Allen wanted to be John Daly. Bennett, who had had a life filled with success and wealth, a happy marriage, two fine sons and a host of friends, had wanted only one thing more—to be famous, and "What's My Line?" had given him that.

They say your life passes before your eyes as you plummet out the window. I have no intention of testing that theory, but when I saw the retrospective "What's My Line?"—an hour of clips from the shows—something very like that happened to me. It wasn't just that my hair went from brunette to blonde and that my clothes went from long to short, it was the storehouse of memories across the years. All that living and laughing and loving recorded on a television show. Who said where has the time gone? I watched it go and was grateful it had gone so well.

10

Among the shows I played in on Broadway while "What's My Line?" was on the air was a revival of *Dinner at Eight,* in which I played Carlotta to Walter Pidgeon's Oliver. I have two reasons for remembering this show rather more vividly than I do most.

The first is that in the play, I was supposed to be arriving from Europe and to have had a terrible time in customs, and to complain bitterly on stage that the customs officer, "Mr. Isadore Goldberg, that son-of-a-bitch," had treated me miserably.

Well, just before curtain time at the opening, Edna Ferber, who had written the play with George Kaufman, came backstage and said, "Arlene, you know George and I wrote this play before Hitler, and in those days you could make jokes like 'Goldberg, that son-of-a-bitch,' but now, well Jews are very sensitive and I don't think it's such a good idea. Can you make it a nice neutral name like Tom Jones or Jack Smith?"

I said I'd try to remember, but opening nights are nerve-laden times, and you have so much on your mind, and she said she understood, but if I possibly could . . .

The way the scene went, I entered, and Walter was at the opposite side of the stage. He was to greet me with "Carlotta!" and my line was "Oliver!" and then we were supposed to embrace. All the way to the stage from my dressing room I kept saying to myself *"Don't say Isadore Goldberg, don't say Isadore Goldberg,"* right up to the point where I made my entrance.

"Carlotta!" said Walter.

"Isadore!" said I, and we embraced as he muttered in my ear, "Whatthehellwasallthatabout?"

The second reason I remember that show in particular is that the entire cast appeared as mystery guests on "What's My Line?" and I failed to guess who they were. So much for all that much-vaunted radar.

Theater audiences are quite different from television audiences. For example, I could play *Dinner at Eight* with a patch on my eye (which I was forced to do for a while), and the audience accepted that as part of my costume or my characterization without any explanation of why I was wearing it. I mean, no program note said, "Miss Francis cut her cornea, eye patch courtesy of Elizabeth Arden." I remember José Ferrer telling me that he had burned his hand just before the opening of *Othello,* in which he played Iago, and had worn a black glove over his bandage. One reviewer, apparently the only one who noticed it, mentioned that he thought it a wonderfully sinister touch, adding even greater villainy to the villainous role.

Television, however, is something else. Any deviation from the norm, from what the audience expects—even a change of hairstyle—brings on a torrent of mail, so that when I appeared with that eye patch I was snowed under by a barrage of letters. Most of them were "oh you poor thing" expressions, and there were a few "Whassa big idea, you showing off or something?" letters, and of course the comics wrote in with some variation of the same joke, "Well well well! If it isn't the girl in the Hathaway shirt!" Television audiences don't like their performers fiddling around with themselves. They want them to stay predictable and recognizable, and they are *very* possessive!

I had to wear the eye patch (and I've had to wear it on several occasions) because of a series of accidents—so many that I became eye-shy and still am. That also explains why I often wear tinted glasses—to protect me against the kind of mishaps I seem to attract (in addition to which I have a few stupid allergies and tremendous sensitivity to dust and pollen and tomatoes and scotch and lobster and you name it, I'm allergic to it). Goodness knows, I don't wear them because I'm afraid of being recognized!

The first accident to my eye came about because my son, Peter, was sitting on my lap, watching a Disney cartoon on television and something in the movie scared him. He turned to bury his head in my shoulder, at the same time lifting his hand, and the scratch on my cornea to which I referred was the result.

A second accident happened when I was reading a telegram while cradling a phone between my shoulder and cheek. The phone slipped and the hand holding the wire automatically went up to catch it while my head went forward, giving me a paper cut across the iris, so painful that I passed out. And a third time, I had a maid who came in one night with a very severe case of shingles. A short time later, I was playing in *Pal Joey* in Denver, and I developed a horrendous pain in my left eye. I rushed to a local doctor who examined it very carefully and couldn't find any foreign matter there to account for the pain. With a thoughtful look on his face he said, "By any chance have you been around anyone with shingles?" I couldn't even *remember* at first, but when I did and told him about the maid, he said yes, that was it, I had herpes in my eye. Excruciating! Is it any wonder I'm fanatically protective of my eyes? It began to seem to me at one point that debris of all sorts have a holding position in the air, just waiting for the man in the control tower to tell them when it's their turn to zero in on my magnetic brown orb.

The eye accidents, however, were nothing compared to a series of disasters which had me thinking I was the Jonah of all time.

The first happened while I was in Westport, acting in a summer stock production. As I would be away for several weeks, it seemed a felicitous time to have our New York apartment thoroughly cleaned.

They had taken the air conditioner out of my bedroom window, leaving a gaping hole which the maid covered with a turkish towel. To secure the towel, the maid had rested it on the casing which had held the air conditioner, and pinioned it with dumbbells with which I exercised. While the shutters were being cleaned, the dumbbells became dislodged, one falling into the room and the other out of the window through the opening.

We live on the eighth floor, and our bedroom windows

were directly over the canopy of a famous restaurant, Le Pavillon, out of which a man and his wife had just emerged. The man was standing outside the canopy, the dumbbell hit him, and he was dead on arrival at the hospital. I have put these facts down coldly because, even now, so many years later, the recollection is still so painful that I have to pretend to myself that I am talking about something that happened to somebody else.

I was called in Westport, and I came into New York immediately, shattered and unbelieving, and covered with guilt. The latter was not because anyone was trying to attach any blame to me, but it *was* my room, they *were* my dumbbells, and I couldn't help feeling that, however inadvertently, I had been responsible for somebody's death.

There would be a trial of course, and it was not financial fear that gripped me, for we were insured—most professional people are; but I couldn't stop thinking about the wife of the man, what her feelings must have been when she saw her husband killed before her eyes—after a gala lunch, most probably, on their holiday in New York. I wrote to her, told her how devastated I was, that I would do anything in my power to help her, although I was sure that nothing I could do would compensate for her loss.

She wrote a very kind, understanding letter to me, but a few days later I had a call from an attorney, telling me that the niece of the man who had been killed was in New York, and that she would like to see me. His tone was friendly, but I was concerned about seeing anyone connected with the family before the trial, and I consulted my agent, who happened also to be a lawyer, about what I ought to do. "See her," he counseled me, "but in my office."

I was trembling when I got to his office, and this charming woman and her husband were already there. "These nice people," I told myself, "can't possibly mean me any harm." I was right.

"Miss Francis," the woman said, "I asked to see you because I know how dreadful you feel. I saw your letter to my aunt, and I wanted you to know that the reason I am here is that in my hometown, my doctor told me I had only a few months to live. We had come to New York that time with my uncle and aunt to consult with someone else, to see if something could possibly be done for me. That's why we were all here. I have just learned that my case was incorrectly diagnosed and that there is nothing at all wrong with me—so I wanted you to know that while one life was taken on that trip, another was given back."

I absolutely went to pieces—I cannot remember a more emotionally charged moment in my life, and I will cherish it forever.

It wasn't long after that when another monumental accident happened to me, and it too involved the taking of someone's life. I was driving back from Long Island on a slippery-when-wet road (although why we, the richest country in the world, should have roads that are slippery when wet I cannot understand). A fine drizzle kept falling, fogging up the windshield, and with every car on the road tailgating the car in front of it, it would have been literally impossible to exceed a speed of thirty or thirty-five miles an hour. The car in front of me somehow skidded, and I stepped on my brake, which sent me skidding myself, straight across the divider to the other side, where I hit a car coming from the opposite direction, and for all I knew at the time, it was instant death for me.

When I regained a degree of consciousness, I was dimly aware of being surrounded by police, and of being loaded into another vehicle. I had no idea where I was. I could see what seemed like hundreds of police and ambulance lights turning, and miles and miles of cars, as well as tons of wreckage. I had a sense of disaster without knowing the cause of it, and I was totally unaware of my torn clothes and of the blood all over me.

I certainly knew nothing of the fact that my skidding car had cost a woman her life.

When Martin was notified, he called our doctor, Ed Goodman, who said, "Don't give the hospital out there permission to do anything—I'm sending an ambulance out to take her into town to Presbyterian Hospital" (on whose staff he was chief surgeon). Physically all I had was a concussion, a broken collarbone, cracked ribs and of course cuts and bruises wherever one looked, but mentally and emotionally I was just about ready for an institution. Think of it—in a comparatively short span of time, I had been involved, however accidentally, in the deaths of two people. If you have as much respect for human life as I have—for any kind of life, come to think of it—that's a terribly difficult thing to live with, and all the assurances in the world from people who loved me that none of it was my fault couldn't erase the overwhelming burden of *mea culpa*.

An accident of this nature, in addition to the sorrow it caused, could very well have had the effect of bankrupting us. Lawsuits were immediately filed against me, naturally, but the *amount* for which I was being sued I found astonishing, to say the least—one and a half million dollars!

A jury was selected, and though we were insured, it was certainly not for anything even approximating that sum. The reason I was worried had nothing to do with my culpability in the matter, but with the fact that it has been explained to me that there are certain lawyers (not all of them by any means) who would not be above making capital of the fact that I am an actress (translation; lives high, probably given to drink), that my earnings are considerable (translation; what's a million and a half to her?), and so on.

One thing militated in my favor. A witness came forth, got on the stand and said, "I was *there* and I can vouch for the fact that the car in front of Miss Francis had skidded, and that she was forced to step on her brake, and that was what resulted in her own skid." He was the *only* person in the whole world who could have so testified, because his car had been exactly alongside of mine and he had seen what had happened. That was the deposition he had given to the police at the time of the accident, and that was what he said on the witness stand, and no amount of trying by the lawyers for the plaintiffs could get him to alter his story in the slightest detail.

The lawyer who represented us had been assigned by the insurance company; he took us aside after our witness had told his story and said, "They're ready to settle rather than see this trial through."

I was thoroughly shaken up. "Settle?" I asked. "But I'm not *guilty* of anything. What is there to *settle?*"

He looked at me as a patient father might regard a rather naive child. "It doesn't matter, Miss Francis," he said, "whether you're guilty or not. Because of *who* you are, that jury out there is going to say, 'She can afford it,' and they'll make them a big award."

Very reluctantly I agreed to a settlement—and the reluctance had nothing to do with how I felt about the survivors. Certainly I felt terribly sorry for them, and I didn't want them to suffer any financial hardship, but on the other hand, making a settlement seemed to me to be a tacit admission that I had been guilty in some way of the death of that poor woman. I shall always feel that this hangs over me, and I still think it's a poor system that permits such settlements as a matter of course.

So much for the bad news. Now the good news. I've mentioned the hate mail performers get, but I want to emphasize the love mail here. This time I don't mean love letters, just loving letters. If you have something which strikes a responsive chord in an audience—if you are Dinah Shore or Lucille Ball or Bob Hope, American institutions who have become part of people's families—those families are going to rally around you, as your own family would, when you need them.

When that happened to me, it was absolutely sensational! The mail that poured in during those two traumatic experiences (and during the minor ones too, but these were special), overwhelmed me. Had it not been for that, and of course for the tremendous support of Martin and Peter (but I would have *expected* that, and probably discounted their reassurances), I hate to think what would have happened to me.

Every now and then I'm accused of sounding like Pollyanna, but I can't help that. I *am* a closet Pollyanna, if the truth be known, and the reason is that enough miracles have happened to make me so. The thousands of prayer cards from Roman Catholics and letters from people of all faiths which told me they were praying for me—what can I say? I believe with all my heart that those vibrations got through to me. And to God. I *have* to believe in the healing quality of that kind of positive love being transmitted through the air, because it did happen to me. It brought me from the very depths of despair, from a depression I didn't think I could come out of, to being myself again. I don't want to hear a single word from you, Alexander Hamilton, about "Your people, Sir, are a great beast." Your people, Sir, are dynamite as far as I'm concerned, and no, I'm not going to run for Congress.

Which reminds me, by the way, that somebody up in Westchester County where we vote actually *did* ask me to run for Congress once. I told the committee that approached me, "How can I possibly do that? I'm on 'What's My Line?,' on the 'Home' show every day, and there's my nighttime show, and I couldn't possibly give them up because that's how I earn my living. I wouldn't want to be a part-time Congresswoman, and I'm just too busy to be anything else."

"Well," they said, "but what about sometime in the future when you're not so busy?"

"Don't be silly," I replicd. "When I'm not so busy you won't want me."

They laughed and assured me that they would, and I don't mean to point or anything like that, but I'm not so busy now and where are they?

To get back to accidents, the things that happened to me directly, such as the monkey biting my finger, always had their comic aspects no matter how uncomfortable they made me. For instance, on a national television show called "Home" (another non-stop series of unplanned insanities that could only happen on live television), we did a program once from Steeplechase Park in Coney Island. It's been torn down now, but in its day Steeplechase Park with its heart-in-the-mouth rides, fun houses, crazy mirrors and the rest was what kids did for kicks instead of smoking pot, and I'm all for bringing it back. Anyway, I was supposed to wander around the place with a microphone in my hand, explaining what everything was to the television viewers. As was always true when we did a remote, we had to bring tons of equipment with us, so there were cables and wires and dollies all around. I was being very careful, threading my way around them, because of my propensity for falling flat on my face. This time it wasn't going to happen!

"This," I said smiling charmingly, "is the moving floor that I'm standing on. Of course it isn't moving *now*. . . ." and I got the signal from the director to start walking toward the railing, which I was supposed to hold on to when it *did* start moving. Something happened to their timing, and before I got to where I was supposed to stand to explain the fun and frolic, the floor started up and I was thrown over the rail. So there I was again—sirens blaring, ambulance lights flashing, and for the next several months I played the show with my leg in a cast, for I'd broken it in several places. It must have been a welcome relief to our audience not to see me with a patch on my eye.

Another rather vivid memory I have has to do with a play called *Mrs. Dally Takes a Lover*, in which I had to wear several wigs. (I also had to learn how to play "After You've Gone" on a slide trombone, but that's another story.) Anyway, on opening night, in a scene where I was supposed to open the door to empty the garbage bin, the kitchen door got stuck, and I tried to yank it open. I was a shade too successful, for not only did it come open, it bonked me in the head, and had it not been for that wig, I'd have been totally knocked out. As it was I was only partially so, and I had enough presence to know that I had to make it to my next line, though at that moment I thought it might be my last.

I'm grateful for the discipline the theater teaches. It enabled me to get through that night. I've known dancers to finish a ballet movement with a broken ankle, and actors who have played scenes perfectly with raging fevers so that they had no idea what they were saying, and it was that way with me that night. I got a lot of applause, because the audience knew something had happened, and the applause was for what they considered to be gallantry. It wasn't gallantry at all. I didn't know what I was doing, I was operating out of instinct. Like a good girl, I waited until I got home to pass out, and it was just a baby concussion that time.

If I were to stop to think about all that (and I hardly dare), I'd have to conclude that it's a wonder I'm still around in one piece. Either I'm the world's champion physical incompetent, *or*—if Sigmund Freud was right in saying there is no such thing as an accident—my unconscious desire is to be unconscious!

11

In 1953, Sylvester (Pat) Weaver was the genius-in-residence at NBC. He had a master plan for the network, which was designed around three blockbuster shows, "Today," intended to catch the early morning viewers, "Tonight," for the insomniacs, and "Home" for the middle of the day. "Today" and "Tonight" have become American Institutions, continuing to hog the lion's share of the TV audience at those hours, and they are both a tremendous tribute to Pat Weaver's foresightedness. "Home," alas, died an untimely death after four years.

In my opinion, its demise was undeserved because (also in my opinion) it was the most innovative, the most carefully thought out and prepared, and it offered the greatest variety of the three. And if anyone thinks that this is a prejudiced report based on the fact that I was the hostess, they're right. I *know* how much work and careful planning went into "Home," and I think we offered our listeners a most generous cornucopia of talent and information. (To say nothing of a lot of unscheduled laughs which I'll get around to.)

Mistress of Ceremonies doesn't accurately describe my job on "Home."

The format of the show was designed as a living magazine, so my official designation was Editor-in-Chief. As in a magazine (and this was the first of its kind on television, I might add), there were various departments; the arts, profiles on people in the news, cooking, sewing, current events, health, gardening, etc., all presided over by experts in their field. We were on the tube five days a week, and we were an hour-long program in the beginning (later extended to an hour and a half), so it took a lot of preparation in advance.

All in all, between "What's My Line?" and various other commitments I had in addition to "Home," I was on a rugged schedule. Added to which, "Home" often took us tootling around the country, and sometimes even the world—so that part of the time I was too busy to run my *own* home.

Martin was up to his erroneous zones as well, and so we were concerned that we weren't spending as much time as we should have liked to spend with Peter. He was past the nurse-maid age, and he needed more absorbing entertainment than playing in the sandpile in the playgrounds of Central Park.

We did try to compensate for not being around all the time by being totally present when we were there. We told ourselves it was the *quality* rather than the quantity of our presence which mattered, and that a lot of parents we knew who were on the premises *all* the time were more remote from their children than we were from Peter. Peter, we felt, under-stood the logistics of our work schedules perfectly, and if he was ever hurt or felt abused or neglected, he never said so.

It is possible, of course, that he was just too decent to let us know how he felt, because decency is one of the qualities he has always had. As an illustration, at one of his birthday par-ties—his eighth—one of the guests arrived an hour early. Her mother had an errand to run and had simply dropped her daughter off at our door, where she stood covered in an ag-ony of embarrassment.

"I'm sorry to be so early, Peter," she said, barely able to look at him.

"You're not early, Linda," he replied. "Everyone else is late." I had him pegged immediately for the diplomatic ser-vice.

Theatrical parents, or any parents who are in the public eye for one reason or another, must always be aware that their children may be subjected to cruel teasing because of them. The result is that many of us bend over backwards, I think, trying to be nonchalant about our profession, but it hardly ever works.

(Which reminds me that as of this writing, there has been a good deal of publicity regarding the fact that the President's daughter, Amy, is attending a public school in Washington.

While I don't want to seem to be equating the Martin Gabels with the Jimmy Carters, I rather imagine that the Carters, in sending her there, are partly motivated by the desire to let Amy know she's just like the other kids on the block. My advice, Mr. President, Mrs. Carter, is to forget it. It won't work. Peter went to public school too, but he knew perfectly well that we weren't in the shoe business, and Amy knows *you* have a special job too, especially with all those Secret Service men sitting outside her classroom.)

Peter would have had to be retarded not to know that his mother's face was all over the place on TV, and that his father was appearing in one play after another on Broadway, and he certainly wasn't that. The fact is that although he went to a public school, it happened to be Hunter Experimental, which was geared to high-IQ kids in those days, and he'd had to pass a stiff examination to get in. I recall an interview that Martin gave to Earl Wilson at the time, in which Earl asked, "Is it true that your son is really a genius?"

The magnificent Mr. Gabel replied, "As they say in racing, if you have a good mare, she never drops a bad foal." Snort snort.

Several years after all of this, by the way, when Peter was all grown up, I asked him whether our visibility when he was in school had been a problem to him, and he said, "As a matter of fact, it was just the opposite. The name 'Arlene Francis' got me some very respectful attention from the kids in my class!" In spite of that reassuring statement (which I didn't entirely believe), I had the feeling it wasn't all that easy for him, growing up under these rather special circumstances, and I worried about his not having more "normal" surroundings. Growing up in Manhattan can be a mixed blessing. While the city offers unique advantages, it isn't a place where children play in the street with other children from the neighborhood and get called in to dinner from the window! Having playmates becomes a project, and Peter had to be shepherded around town to the homes of schoolmates, or they came to ours—and that involved a shepherd or two, too.

At that time we were living in a townhouse, and that meant we had to have a couple on the premises at all times, to handle the work and to watch out for Peter when we were not there. We called employment agencies, explained our needs, and the parade began.

We interviewed couples who, as they came into the house, eyed the stairs and were aghast there was no elevator. Others threw their hands up in horror at the mention of a child. There was one couple that would work only four days a week, and we surmised that at the salary they were asking, they needed the other three days to look after their own country estate. Then there were some who could clean but not cook/cook but not clean, or couldn't do either but were willing to try. It was all terribly discouraging.

And suddenly, piercing the miasma of gloom which all of that had thrown me into, a man and his wife walked into the house and instinctively I felt the problem was solved. They seemed absolutely ideal. They were both handsome people, they were obviously qualified to do all that needed to be done in our house, and they were, above all, eager to please. I told them that they would hear from me as soon as I had checked their references, smiled encouragingly, and expected them to take their leave. Instead of that, Stephen, the husband, asked if I would object to calling the man whose number he had given me, while they were present. It seemed like an odd request, but he sounded rather urgent and I reasoned to myself that they were probably badly in need of a job and wanted to know whether they had one. That was true, but not quite as I had written the scenario. It could also have been true that a confederate was waiting at the other end of the line to give a false reference—such things *do* happen—but that wasn't so either.

It was a very shaken Arlene Francis who listened attentively to a prison correction officer who told me what there was to know about Stephen and Ivy, the attractive people who stood before me, watching my facial expressions anxiously.

Well they might, for I was hearing that Stephen had served a stiff jail sentence for assault with a deadly weapon against a fellow serviceman, but that he had been, quote, rehabilitated, unquote, and had been working in the home of the correction officer, in the country, for a year, behaving in an exemplary way. He had married a lovely woman, was completely trustworthy and was in fact an outstanding example of what the prison system is capable of accomplishing when it sets its mind to it! The officer felt that Stephen had paid his debt to society and deserved a chance.

My mind raced around as I replaced the receiver. How

many times had I said publicly that people who had done time had never been given a chance to go straight? That it was a vicious circle where nobody was willing to take the risk of employing someone with a record? People, not platforms, must reach out, I had said—take hold, educate and *care*.

The lip service I had paid now challenged me to put my money where my principles were. There was a long silence between us. "Look here," I said, "my husband and I have only one thing of real value in this house, our son. Mr. X tells me you were marvelous with his children, and I am going to give you the opportunity to work here and help us look after Peter. I am putting my trust in you. Shall we shake hands on that?" His pretty wife cried, and I was shattered for the rest of the day.

Stephen and Ivy moved in the following Monday and I didn't look back for two years. They seemed the answer to all our problems, for Ivy was warm and dear and an excellent cook, while Stephen drove for us, did the heavy cleaning and odd jobs around the house. This, however, was the least of what he did for us. The most important thing he did was to become a companion to Peter. He'd go out in the park and play baseball with him, he taught him how to box, he had an easy big-brother manner—he was, in short, absolutely ideal and Peter adored him.

The feeling was reciprocated, I felt, for I remember that when Peter had to go to the hospital to have his tonsils out, Stephen said to me "u-h-uh—I'm not going to let that kid spend a night in a hospital alone," and sure enough, he made them put up a cot in Peter's hospital room and he spent the night on it. What a sense of security it gave us! We considered ourselves the luckiest people in the world.

Suddenly there were storm warnings. Small amounts of cash would disappear. I admit to having been somewhat careless about leaving money about in a desk drawer or on a dresser—not large amounts, to be sure—and I never thought of it as a temptation. When "Person to Person" moved into our house with its cameras, lights and equipment, the large crew which had to handle it all had the run of our house. After they left, $500 that I kept in a strongbox for emergencies also left. Without sounding or feeling in the least accusatory, I explained my dilemma to Stephen, as one would to a trusted friend, and he proceeded to turn the house upside down in an effort to find the missing money. He even scolded me mildly, saying that I was too careless with money, and that probably I had put it somewhere else. Needless to say, it didn't turn up.

In their second year with us, Ivy had a baby, and I arranged to get them an apartment in a new housing development. Ivy stayed with her baby, and Stephen's time became less dependable with us, for he had to go back and forth, so I suggested that he find a different job, a day job which would not tie him down and keep him from Ivy and the baby at night. And he agreed. So readily, in fact, that I had my first glimmering of suspicion about him—but that's all it was, just a glimmering.

A short time after that I had a call from a bank. A Mr. Stephen———had presented them with a check for $3,500 signed by me, and had I written it? I had not, of course. He had forged my name to a personal check he had stolen. The bank stalled him while they sent for the police and that was that.

We knew this would break Peter's heart (indeed, it very nearly broke mine), but on the other hand it was not a matter to which we could close our eyes and pretend nothing had happened. And of course, we had terrible qualms about having to go to court and testify against someone who had lived in our house and who had been a part of our family. I did write a letter to the judge asking him to take into consideration the two years of exemplary conduct and service in our home before he pronounced sentence on Stephen. Logical or not, to a sensitive boy like Peter, Stephen's departure constituted a desertion, and the forgery coming on top of that caused him immeasurable pain.

The incident forced Martin and me to sit down, assess the situation, and examine our options. We concluded that an only child of theatrical parents would be better off in boarding school. He was no longer at Hunter Experimental, which went only through the fourth grade, and while he was doing quite well at Trinity, a school on the other side of town from where we lived, he would soon be approaching prep school age, and that, we thought, would be the right time for him to go away. We felt we should prepare him for this eventuality, and when we broached the subject he offered no objections—indeed, he seemed to take it for granted, as some of his friends already were at prep schools in New England. In due course, we started making the rounds.

They all looked terrific to me and to Martin—ivy-covered buildings, broad playing fields filled with bright-eyed, shouting boys who seemed to be having a marvelous time. Certainly they were an improvement over the playing fields of Central Park, and we felt that Peter would blossom in this milieu. We settled on Deerfield Academy in Massachusetts (partly because one of his closest friends, Jonathan Cerf, was also going there—a chum is always a compelling reason for selecting one school over another!). When the time came, we drove Peter up, all three of us making bright conversation during the trip, about how wonderful it was going to be.

We behaved classically, all three of us. We classically walked around the campus, met the Headmaster, oohed and ahhhed about the beauty of the grounds and the buildings and were perfectly charming to all the faculty members we met. Peter classically waved us off as though he could hardly wait to get rid of us, and I classically cried my heart out when we got back into the car. We classically assured each other that we had done the Sensible, Modern Thing, that it was best for Peter to be with boys his own age (albeit he was the youngest one there), and all in all it was like a Hardy Family movie.

We were prepared for the fact that he might be a trifle homesick. ("Remember, Marty? How he was first time he went to camp?" "Yes, but he was much *younger*. Your son's a *man* now. Stop crying!" "I hope you're right, how I *hope* you are! I'm not sure I liked the look on his face when he left . . ." "Really darling, *you're* talking like a child. What if he *is* a little uneasy at first? He'll get over it. Here's my handkerchief. Wipe your mascara.")

Martin notwithstanding, my son the man called me at one in the morning a few weeks after he'd been there, and he was so choked up I could hardly make out what he was saying. "What *is* it darling, Peter dear, please don't cry, what's *happened?*" I asked, full of alarm. "Please tell me, if you've done something terrible, whatever it is, we'll try to help, just *tell* me. . . !"

"It's noth-nothing like that," he replied through sobs, "but we have to get up at six in the morning and it's pitch black out and you have to go into the bathroom and take a shower and it's freezing, and then you have to go b-back and g-get dressed and make your bed and then you go across the campus and it's very dark and you g-go to the refectory for your breakfast and g-go to your first class and my first class is Latin and how'd *you* like to start the day with *Latin?*"

Shades of Mount St. Vincent! As he talked to me, recollections of black stockings and black-robed nuns, cold halls and icy dormitories, rosaries and genuflections, imposed silences and rigorous schedules crowded back into my mind. I remembered how *I* had wanted to run away, and my empathy was so great that I almost told him to pack his clothes and come home. "No, it builds character," I told myself, just as I'm sure my parents must have told *them*selves, and to be honest, I'm still not sure any of us were right. One thing is probably true, however. It would have haunted Peter as a defeat if he'd given up at *that* stage. (At least that's what I keep telling myself, because it's also true that he had a pretty good character to begin with and probably didn't need to have it put to such tests.)

Eventually he accommodated himself to all the things he had complained of, and some time later when we offered him the option of leaving, he refused. I don't think it was that he had gotten all that gung-ho, but he had worked out his own formula for survival in a less-than-ideal situation, which was to get into the rhythm of the place, to find those areas in which he could involve himself, and to participate in the school's activities on many levels.

Of the memorabilia I've hoarded that concern Peter, one of my favorite communications from him is a card, one of the "clever" ones which took the place of the sugary sentimental kind. The printed message on the card reads, "The wonderful success of our relationship is based on a rare and unique combination"—and when you unfolded the card the message continued—"you and me." Peter didn't make that up, but he *did* pick it out, and he sent it to me while I was playing down in Florida, in a comedy by Sam Taylor named *Beekman Place*. His own written message ran: "Dear famous star of stage, screen, television, Louisville, Palm Beach, New York, etc. So you're a big hit as usual. It must get kind of boring. Actually I'm only kidding. I just think you're a better mother than an actress. I am in the Choate debate a week from Friday, and I've got to give an 8-minute speech in front of 500 people at Choate. I'm only the fourth junior to ever be in an outside debate. I'm scared stiff. Get home. Love, love, big love, Peter."

No laurel wreath, no accolade from a critic could have given me the glow of pleasure Peter's letter did, but of even greater moment than his judgment of my performance as a mother, was the relief I felt that he seemed to be enjoying and to have become a part of his school. That, in point of fact, he was enough of a ham to want me to know he hadn't been performing too badly himself!

12

I've sometimes felt that I live in sort of a global village, where the cottage industry is entertainment and the national anthem is Irving Berlin's "There's no business like show business." To the occupants of my village, there's no business *but* show business and no people but show people. We seem all to know each other, and though we don't necessarily all love each other, we do share the same concerns, speak the same language and travel in packs because we feel more comfortable with each other. We're not quite as parochial as we used to be, and most of us now number among our good friends people whom we designate as "civilians," but we are more clannish than people in most other professions.

Some of that is a collective hangover of insecurity, a bequest from the days when theater people were considered by the gentry to be thieves, rogues and vagabonds. I don't even have to go that far back in history—I need only remember my father's attitude about show people. He was straitlaced yes, but he was by no means unique in his generation, which thought our kaleidoscopic world of glitter, make-believe and mirth was an equation for sin and perdition. Our theatrical ancestors, I think, would have been astonished to see the degree of acceptance we have achieved, and to read in columns about our having attended dinner at the White House, had high tea with the Ambassador to Japan and been cheek-by-jowl with the gentry!

(But even though they let us in the front door most places these days, every now and again we get a rude reminder not to get too uppity. There is a rather well known party-giver who had cultivated a highly selective circle of theatrical friends, whom she used to brighten her parties. A few years back, however, she was interviewed by the best society columnist of them all, Aileen Mehle, who writes under the name of Suzy. Aileen asked her whether her annual Christmas ball would again include her celebrity friends, and she replied, "No, I don't ask theater people any more—except, of course, the Joshua Lockwood Logans and the Martin Gabels." If she reads this, I imagine she'll pare her list down to the Joshua Lockwood Logans.)

When we gave parties or went to them in the early days of our marriage, it was a way of keeping tabs on the clan. We lived irregular lives, kept irregular hours and went scooting around the world to work, so any occasion was an excuse for a party, a way of reaffirming our place in a peripatetic community. If Irwin and Marian Shaw came to New York from Paris, where they lived, we gave a party. If Harry Kurnitz came from London where *he* lived for a while, we gave a party. If somebody was leaving town to do a picture, we gave a party. If somebody had just had a book published or a play optioned or had been signed to write a score—we gave a party. Any excuse to foregather in celebration of each other.

The parties have a different ambience today and they include lots of people not connected with the arts (unless you consider politics an art, making money an art, etc.), and while it's gratifying to meet wheelers and dealers, movers and shakers from other worlds, somehow nothing seems to compare with my own familiar, cozy, extraverted world.

Entertainment at those early parties was spontaneous and joyful. You didn't even have to drop a hat to get composers to sit down to play their new scores or their old hits, to get singers to sing, or comedians to do their routines. Performers like to perform, and they like best of all to perform for other performers, because nobody appreciates it more. Creative people are the greatest audience on earth, and that's why every party in those days was a hit revue no producer would have been able to finance with such stars. Frank Loesser, Abe Burrows, Arthur Schwartz, Harold Rome, Julie Styne—whoever was there was happy "to oblige," or to accompany the likes of Ethel Merman, Beverly Sills, Comden and Green and you name them.

One unforgettable memory is of a party we gave when we lived in that tiny house in the East Seventies. It had a curved staircase from the downstairs dining room to the upstairs living room, and a rather wide landing at the curve, big enough to accommodate our small grand piano. At this particular party, Harold Arlen, composer of the *Wizard of Oz* score, among myriad others, sat at the piano, and about seventy-five guests were seated on the floor, on the steps, and hanging over the railing down from the upper bedrooms. Topside was Peter in his Dr. Denton pajamas, and like everyone else, he was listening in hushed silence to Judy Garland as she sang "Somewhere Over the Rainbow" in her heart-breaking voice.

There were other parties that were memorable, but not always because of the entertainment. One such we gave at 375 Park Avenue, before it got the wrecking ball from Seagrams. Our apartment was a duplex and the elevator opened directly into our foyer. Naturally the elevator men were extremely careful about whom they brought up, but sometimes when a big party was in progress and guests were apt to arrive in groups, the rules were somewhat relaxed.

To this party we had invited Herman Levin, who was an old Philadelphia buddy of Martin's and the producer of *My Fair Lady*. When he came off the elevator with a group of other gala, black-tied gentlemen and begowned ladies, we assumed that they were *My Fair Lady* backers whom Herman had brought along, knowing that it was to be a big party and feeling we wouldn't mind. (*Attention future guests:* Phone first.)

The festive little group of unknowns was jolly enough, and they blended into the scenery with no trouble, making their way upstairs to my bedroom at some point in the evening, presumably to avail themselves of the facilities. (Not in a group, of course. One at a time.) They also availed themselves of several bottles of unopened perfume (including a giant bottle of Joy, not the dishwashing lotion, the real-McCoy zillion-dollars-an-ounce perfume by Jean Patou) and all my jewelry.

We didn't know it had happened until the party was over, and naturally, when we discovered it, we rejected the possibility that we had been ripped off by any of our guests. And suddenly it dawned on us (with a little prodding from the police) that there were some people at the party we didn't know—the group who had come with Herman. But *surely* Herman's friends—no, impossible! Nevertheless we called him, and it wasn't until he said "Who? Who?" that we realized they hadn't come with him. The police later explained about this well-known (except to us, apparently) racket. Party crashers, they explained, travelled in packs like wolves, stood outside of affluent buildings, waited for somebody in party clothes to arrive, and then got into the same elevator, seemingly by chance. If it turned out to be a small party, a sit-down dinner or something of that nature, they could always apologize and say they'd gotten off at the wrong floor or were in the wrong building or whatever, and as they were invariably well-dressed and well-spoken, there was usually a reluctance to challenge them.

Another evening I remember, but this one with pleasure, was a party given for Moss Hart by Random House, in honor of the publication of his remarkable autobiography, *Act One*. Now when somebody gives a party in your honor, the usual reaction is to dig your toe in the sand and be grateful, modest and shy, but that wasn't Moss's style. He had written his first book, and by gum he wanted that party to be a smash, so he did what came naturally to him: he directed it. And Moss was a tough director—that's why he had so many hits—so when he called rehearsals, you'd better rehearse. He gave out assignments for material to be written, cast the party-goers who would act and sing, and then rehearsed us all in our routines with the same dedication that he would have expended on a major Broadway revue.

I was part of a chorus quartette (the other members being Phyllis Cerf, Kitty Carlisle Hart and Florence Rome) who sang a parody of Cole Porter's "You're The Tops," which was written for the occasion by Harold Rome, and even on the morning of the evening of the soiree, Moss herded us all down to Mamma Leone's cellar, where the party was to be held, for a last rehearsal. We griped a lot, dragging ourselves there at the crack of dawn with our hair in rollers and scarves tied around our heads, but nobody could say no to Moss. "All right, ladies," said our glorious leader, "One, a, two, a three, a . . ." and we ladies of the ensemble began:

"You're the tops!" (*Point finger at audience*)

"You're a borscht patatah . . ." (*Arms above head*)
"You're the tops . . ." (*Turn sideways*)
"You're a Lindy's waitah . . ." (*Kick*)
Etc. etc. etc.

There were many other songs and dozens of sketches (including one with a cast which included the honoree himself, plus Martin, Adolph Green and Bennett Cerf, all dressed as charwomen; a less beguiling group of drag queens has seldom been rounded up in a paddy wagon). At any rate, it was worth all the trouble. Moss got his wish—that this should be one of the best parties ever given. Random House got *its* wish too, that his book should be wildly successful.

Our cozy evenings, which in the beginning had a hard core of participants—Irving Lazar, Eve and George Backer, Irwin and Marian Shaw, Harry Kurnitz, Joan and Arthur Stanton, the Calherns and half a dozen other of our nearest and dearest—began to grow to the point that they were giant rallies. The group enlarged so that every party had seventy-five to a hundred guests, because it was hard to ask the so-and-sos without including the watchamacallits and you wouldn't want to hurt whoozis' feelings.

One such festival was given at the home of the George Axelrods in honor of Irving Lazar, Swifty to his friends, who just happened to be legion and Martin and I are proud to be counted among them. Legion got invitations that said "Swifty is Fifty," which after all these years I am prepared to admit was a fraud. It wasn't his birthday, but it seemed like a good idea at the time, and once again Moss was in charge—assigning material to be written, casting the performers. It was only right that Moss should do this, since he had been Swifty's first major client, although by the time of the party, the list included some of the most talented people around. They wrote the material, which of course centered around Swifty—his personal appearance (a five-foot-three bald bundle of dynamite), his personal foibles (Mr. Clean incarnate), and his lifestyle (betcha my Picasso can lick your Picasso). It was good-natured and all done with enormous affection, and I particularly remember the parody which Comden and Green wrote to Irving Berlin's "The Girl That I Marry," which dealt with all of the above characteristics. Betty sang it as though she were Irving's lovelorn secretary to whom he never paid any

31. Moss Hart's *Act One* party rehearsal—l. to r., Kitty Carlisle Hart, Phyllis Cerf, Florence Rome, me.

32. *Act One* party—the beauties, l. to r., are Martin, Adolph Green, Bennett Cerf and Moss Hart.

33

33. "Swifty Is Fifty"—some of the all-star audience.
34. "Swifty Is Fifty" party. The performers, l. to r.—Martin, me, Joan
Axelrod, Kitty Hart, George Axelrod, Moss.

34

35

35. The slim dark-haired gentleman singing with me is none other than Mike Douglas. The band was called the Central Park Zoo, and the hot guitar, upper left, is being played by Peter Gabel. The smiling electronic pianist is Jonathan Cerf.
36. With Jerry Lewis on the set of "Home."
37. Helen Keller "listening" to me on the "Home" show.
38. With Carl Sandburg on his plantation in North Carolina.
39. With Judge Joseph Welch, in Boston, on "Home."

36

37

38

39

attention. (He was a bachelor at the time, but has since been matrimonially tamed by lovely chic Mary.)

> *The girl that he marries will have to be*
> *As small as the Baroness de Bouillerie*
> *As tall as Miss Bacall*
> *And she'll know her Picassos from holes in the wall:*
> *Slim Hayward, Sweet Kitty, rolled into one*
> *Yet the soul of a hooker when day is done:*
> *At their wedding while he's heading*
> *Down the aisle, turkish towels she'll be spreading*
> *A girl sanitary*
> *The girl that he'll marry must be.*

(The Baroness de Bouillerie, it should be noted, stood four-foot-eleven. And "Sweet Kitty" could be no other than the sweetest Kitty there is—Kitty Carlisle Hart.)

When everyone had performed, Swifty got up to say *his* piece. We were prepared for something touching and sentimental—even though it would have been out of character. We got it. We were all silent, as he brushed a tear from his eye. "I want you all to remember," he said, "—I made you, and I can break you!"

There was a supper at our house on 64th Street (we seem to have moved every three years—something Freudian, I guess) one Sunday night in honor of Rex Harrison and his lovely bride, Kay Kendall. (When they arrived, I remember she had about a hundred dollars worth of loose flowers in her arms which she thrust at me. "For you, for you my dearest one!" she said in that restrained way she had, and I ungratefully thought, "Where in the devil am I going to get enough vases for these?" while I said aloud, "You *shouldn't* have!" and meant every word of it.)

It was a rollicking group, and we had invited some jazz musicians who shall be nameless for reasons which will be apparent. Now then, there may be hostesses who do this kind of thing—buffets for fifty—effortlessly, but I regret to say that I am not among them. Even when I don't do all the cooking—which I didn't for this one, though I did *some* of it—there are still a million and one details to be seen to, and I don't like to leave things to chance. ("Chance" in this case being a rather inefficient part-time maid who had agreed to give up her Sunday off in return for a sizable block of AT&T plus carfare.) At any rate, I'd worked all day setting up the buffet table and checking out those details. Enough ice? check. Enough glasses? check. Enough booze? check. Enough towels in the bathroom? check. New bars of soap? check. Enough cigarettes? check. Oh God! I forgot the nuts! That sort of thing. By the time the guests had arrived, I was exhausted.

None of that would have mattered if I'd been able to relax after dinner and enjoy those interesting people we'd assembled, but the problem was that I had to get over to the studio to do "What's My Line?" I was sort of dragging myself around, and one of those jazz musicians, noticing my fatigue, came over to me and said, "Listen Arlene, I can see how tired you are, but I've got this terrific pill that'll keep you going. It gives you a lot of energy when you need it. Try it, why don't you? It can't hurt." Sport that I was, I said, "Why not?" and popped my first and last upper into my mouth.

What I say here is simply hearsay and surmise, because I can't remember a thing. I *assume* I got to the show all right, at least I've never heard that I didn't. I also assume that I got through the program without any major disasters. The only thing I recall is sitting on a sofa in my apartment later and wondering who all those people were. Phyllis and Bennett Cerf had brought me home in this, what is now called "spaced-out" condition. What I can't figure out is why anyone would try to get that way deliberately.

We interrupt this account of mad revels to explain why Martin and I no longer live on 64th St., although it was one of the most attractive apartments in New York.

When last we left Stephen and Ivy, they were on their way to the pokey, and had been replaced by a Russian couple named—you'll never believe this—Nicholas and Alexandra. Nicholas was no less regal than the Romanoff of the same name but Alexandra was somewhat humbler—at least I didn't get the feeling that she was condescending when she spoke to me, which I often did with Nicholas.

Now we add to this cast an Indian guru named Yogi Vithaldis, a splendid man who used to come to the apartment a few times a week to give me and two actress friends of mine, Joan Alexander Stanton and Phyllis Adams Jenkins, lessons in yoga. Yogi Vithaldis, I will admit, presented an interesting picture as he trundled over to the house in his gauze drawers (dhotis, I believe they are called), long tunic, turban and heavy brown shoes, but he was a fine figger of a man and a marvelous teacher. We wore leotards, emptied our minds as he instructed us to, stood on our heads, sat in the lotus position and all the rest. Yoga hadn't become the commonplace it is now, and we were very proud of ourselves for being front runners in the new movement.

One day, Yogi Vithaldis came bearing gifts: an enormous juice extractor, a bunch of carrots and a head of cabbage. Not surprisingly, he was a vegetarian, and I remember that he almost killed my interest in steak forever by saying "Of course, if you wish to dine on the decaying flesh of dead animals, that is your business." This day, he wanted to demonstrate to us how truly delicious the juice of vegetables could be, so we dutifully followed him into the kitchen, all of us looking like Japanese wrestlers in our leotards. Dancing about gleefully, we watched him assemble the machine and start the vegetables juicing, when suddenly there stood my resident czar, looking rather as I imagine the genuine Nicholas must have looked when he caught Rasputin in the act. "Owt . . . *owt awv my keetchen!*" he screamed with strangled outrage, and then followed it up with an outburst in Russian, which under the circumstances I'm rather glad none of us understood. One word I *did* understand—somebody had taught me the Russian word for *mother*, and it seemed to crop up quite often in the stream of vituperation. I can't really believe he was calling us what I *think* he might have been, so I'll settle for thinking he was talking about Mother India.

I was dazed by the performance. Nicholas had always been dependable, and to my knowledge he had never behaved with eccentricity before. I concluded that he had some kind of problem and that he had been driven to unseemly behavior by the sight of three young women jumping up and down in their skivvies. Yogi Vithaldis, a gentle person who shrank from these hostile vibes, left the room with dignity, and I bundled the rest of my shell-shocked guests out of the house with apologies.

As soon as everyone had left, I thought it over, picked up the phone and called a man I knew who was on the board of governors of a certain co-operative hotel. I asked him if there was anything available, and he said yes, there was one quite large apartment, but he warned me that it looked rather like Dresden had looked after the Allies had bombed it. The previous owners had removed all the boiserie walls just for starters, and everything else—I was going to say "that wasn't nailed down," but they'd managed most of that too. Undeterred, I went over that afternoon without saying a word to Martin or anyone else, saw it, nodded, and wrote a substantial check as evidence of my good faith that I intended to buy it.

When Martin came home that evening I asked him how he'd like to live in a hotel. He thought I'd suddenly gone mad, since we both loved our spacious apartment on East 64th Street and it had been understood between us that all things being equal, that would be our happily-ever-after nesting place. I explained to him that the point had been reached where all things were not equal any longer. I was not equal, for example, to hiring and firing people and I refused to live my life by the rules laid down by people who worked for me. I also offered certain enticements, such as that I would personally cook breakfast, and that the hotel was within throwing distance of P. J. Clarke's. His eyes lit up at that, and what with one thing and another he agreed. We've never looked back.

When we had cleared out the debris and gotten our new apartment into shape, we inaugurated it with a party in honor of Harry Kurnitz, newly returned from living in Europe. We asked him for a guest list, which, when we looked it over, we were pleased to see contained only people we knew and liked very much ourselves. Perhaps we wouldn't have asked them all at the same time, as it was a lengthy list, but it was Harry's party and we didn't mind crowding the room a bit for him. For some reason it didn't occur to us that there was another, more trenchant, reason for not asking *all* of these people at the same time, and it didn't dawn on us until they started to arrive. Our wicked friend Harry had given us a list of ex-husbands, ex-wives, current husbands, current wives, ex-lovers, contemplated lovers and the rest of the *la ronde* syndrome. That's what came of living in Paris and London!

Ready everyone? There was publisher Tom Guinzburg

and his *then* wife Rita Gam, and *her* ex-husband Sidney Lumet and *his* then wife Gloria Vanderbilt, and as of *now*, that kit and kaboodle have different partners. Then there was Jason Robards and *his* then wife Lauren Bacall, who had been a former dear and close friend of Frank Sinatra, who was also there, as was another dear and close former friend of his, Adele Beatty and *her* then husband Stanley Donen, and you can scratch all *those* entries as of today too. *And* there was Henry Fonda and *his* then wife, an Italian countess named Afdera, and *his* ex-wife Susan Hammerstein and *her* then husband, Michael Wager and you may forget all those alliances now too. AND there was Joan Alexander Stanton and her husband Arthur Stanton, who *had* been married to Joan Axelrod, who was there with her husband George. There were even sisters who weren't speaking at the time, such as Irene Selznick and Edie Goetz, and all it needed was Bennett Cerf and Leonard Lyons, one of the better-known feuds of the day, so of course they were both there too.

Everyone was terribly civilized, as though they'd been invented by Noel Coward just for the evening, but the tension was there under the surface, and at one point Florence Rome said to me, "Listen Arlene, I'm too nervous to stay. Frank Sinatra has locked himself in the bathroom and refuses to come out and even though I'm dying to know how it all turns out, I haven't the guts to witness it. I'll call you tomorrow."

And through it all, Kurnitz just sat in the corner, smiling benignly like a skinny Buddha, making dry little jokes. Somehow I feel that if he came back now, the first thing he'd want to do is have the same party with all the new partners, and oh, how I wish we could do it for him!

There have been parties we've gone to which classify as spectaculars, not only because of their size but because of their original themes. Truman Capote's highly publicized Black and White Ball (all designed by Evie Backer, by the way), in honor of publisher Katharine Graham was one, and Frank Sinatra's parties, for which he flies a planeful of his friends to his compound at Palm Springs over the Christmas holidays, are in a class by themselves. Kubla Khan never had it so good, for Old Blue Eyes is among the world's most considerate hosts. As a matter of fact, among the most memorable parties I recall was one he gave—although it doesn't really classify as just a "party." It was a vacation, actually.

I must explain that I don't ordinarily have time for vacations. I can't seem to manage them, and I am certainly incapable of *planning* for them. Every time I see a television commercial of Robert Morley persuading me to go to merry England and visit the stately homes, I say, "Why not? I'll do it!" But by the time the message is over, I've put it out of my mind. And all that smooching that takes place in the sexy waters of Jamaica makes a trip to the island very promising, but the siren song eludes me and I choose to skinny-dip in my own Mount Kisco pool.

In all my working years I think I've only taken about three serious holidays—and one of those was a yachting cruise down the California coast, engineered and hosted by the aforementioned Francis Albert Sinatra. Over the side he piped Lauren Bacall, Joan and George Axelrod, Gloria and (the late gentle restaurateur) Mike Romanoff, Martin and me.

It was a glorious sea voyage. The ocean was sparkling, the champagne was sparkling, the talk—well, if it wasn't exactly sparkling, it was certainly a cut above your run-of-the-mill group therapy sessions. As the night of July 3 came to a rather tiddly end, Frank admonished us all not to have a drink before lunch the next day . . . no Bloody Marys to correct hangovers—nothing! We were to meet at 12:30 on the afterdeck, where a small ceremony would take place in honor of our country.

How much do any of us really know about the private feelings of public personalities? They entertain us and if they are good, we applaud. If they are superstars (and Sinatra has to be considered the most super of them all) we either enjoy or are incensed by the glut of columns purporting to print all the news that's fit. The only gossip that's worth the price paid for it is a disaster item, often cruel, out of context or untrue.

I am not going to write a paean of praise to Frank Sinatra. He doesn't need me for that. He's already more than paid his dues. But I do want to tell you it was *he* who thought of arranging our Fourth of July celebration; it was *he* who got up early and, with Martin, went through all the books and magazines on board to find some appropriate verses along with the Preamble to the Constitution to read to us; it was *he* who, without being sentimental, stated what America meant to him and that he took some extra joy from the fact that an Italian had discovered it.

We stood at attention when the flag was raised, and Jew/Armenian/Russian/Italian, all-American saluted it proudly. "We the people of the United States"—only eight of us present there—paying our grateful respects. How many do you know who did the same, on whatever scale *they* could afford?

One more on my list of memorable parties is one given by the Mark Goodsons to celebrate the Gabels' twenty-eighth wedding anniversary. It wasn't just that the basics were impeccable—the food and drink, that is—and that a hundred of our nearest and dearest were present; it was the meticulous working out of the details: material especially written and performed (of the "This is your life Martin and Arlene!" variety, and I hope Mark forgives my using a non-Goodson-Todman title as an example). A flock of pictures from childhood onward (mine, Martin's, Peter's), which Susan and Mark had rounded up with the undercover assistance of my secretary (and friend) Carol Butz, known affectionately to everyone as Bootzie, had been blown up to poster size and covered every inch of wall space. The pictures with hand-printed captions reproduced in this book are examples. It was the party of *that* year.

Another marvelous anniversary party (on our thirty-first) was given us by our very dear friends Bill and Judy Green. In addition to its being a warm, loving gathering of friends, this party had a few distinguishing features it would be hard to duplicate at most parties, I believe. Never mind that the majority of the guests had driven for more than an hour from Manhattan to get to the Greens' Westchester estate for the occasion. Never mind that I, who have not exactly built my career around being a singer, sang a love song to Martin, written for me by Harold Rome, who accompanied me (part of the lyric went "Near but unreachable/Smart but unteachable/Dumbbell and genius and nut/But/All I've got of/What they loosely call love/Is for Martin . . ."). Never mind that Judy wrote a song for us to a tune by Joe Raposo and that *he* accompained *her* as she sang "It isn't easy being Arlene/Having to be a poor Armenian peasant with a dream!" I think all of us present would have to admit that the high spot of the evening was the delicious dinner, cooked for the forty-eight guests by what has to be the most highly paid singing chef in the land, Francis Albert Sinatra. (We all loved hearing him warble later too, but the linguine with clam sauce . . . um-um!)

I can't leave this entertainment series without telling how I got an early lesson in hospitality. I learned it from Neil, back in the days when I was so nervous about being hostess to the Skourases.

This was our first dinner party, and it was made up of friends from radio, mostly—Florence Robinson, Sam Levene, Joan Alexander, several other soap-opera chums, and a few of Neil's associates at Paramount. To impress everyone, I suppose, I had set the table with our most elaborate cloth, which had been a wedding gift. It was hand embroidered, and so exquisite I shuddered at the notion that it could be wounded by a fork or stained by careless spillage. Some miserable demon or other must have been prompting me because, thinking myself very witty indeed, I got up from the table and said, "Now this tablecloth is my favorite present and besides it costs a million dollars to launder, so if you want to spill anything, please do it on the carpet!"

A few embarrassed giggles greeted my gracious words, and Sam Levene got up from the table, spread his napkin on the floor, took his plate and glass and silver and laid them on the napkin, and then sat on the floor. Neil was being served while that happened, and he took the mashed potatoes out of the bowl, spread them on the tablecloth, took the peas and put them in the mashed potatoes and then said, "All right, Sam, you can come back now."

The lesson was basic. If you have objects so precious you can't bear the thought of human beings coming in contact with them, put them under lock and key or go live alone among your treasures. But when you have guests, your first obligation is to make them comfortable. One didn't need Emily Post if one had Neil Agnew.

One more postscript: One of the things that I felt we were able to give Peter, as a result of being in the theater, was a chance to meet a lot of talented and wise people who might serve as an example to him. We felt this to be an advantage which almost made up for our own inability to spend more time with him as "normal" every-day parents might be able to do. When he had grown up, I asked him about his recollections of those parties we gave, whether he remembered any distinguished people who impressed him particularly.

"To tell the truth," he said, "I didn't know they were supposed to be so distinguished, and the people I remember best from those days were Stephen and Ivy." So much for parental know-how.

13

While I was doing the "Home" show, a magazine story appeared in which I was described as "the world's most highly paid saleswoman." I was even presented with an award at a banquet in the Grand Ballroom of the Waldorf Astoria Hotel, all because of my prowess in persuading people to heat their houses with this fuel, or improve their muscle-tone with that breakfast food. (Can you imagine several hundred people foregathering and eating creamed chicken out of patty shells for a reason like that?) In accepting the award, I remember making a few wry comments about my earlier ambition to be "Actress of the Year," had evolved strangely into being "Saleswoman of the Year." Obviously my knack for salesmanship did not extend to selling myself to theatrical producers.

I'd travelled a long road from my first commercial, which had been on behalf of Lydia Pinkham's Vegetable Compound, and shall we skip the comments about obsolescence? I will icily point out that I was only seventeen years old when I did that commercial, and even those who never tried the product may possibly remember a ditty which was popular at the time:

> Oh let us sing of Lydia Pinkham,
> The benefactress of the human race,
> She invented a vegetable compound
> Now the papers all print her face.

At any rate, my voice then was as low as it is now, and the message I had to deliver was something along these lines:

I am a woman forty years old, and I ran a terrible house. Dishes were piled high in the sink, there were newspapers all over the floor,

I walked around all day in an old bathrobe, my hair was a mess, and life was a daily horror. I didn't like my husband and he didn't like me. Then [*big pause, change of tone*] I took Lydia Pinkham's Vegetable Compound. I am now the mother of four beautiful children and the life of the party.

All right, those *weren't* the exact words, but it is the exact spirit which had to be conveyed, and after I had been on the air with that commercial for a few weeks, Charles Pinkham, the president, came down from Boston where the Lydia Pinkham company was based. When he asked to see me, I was a little scared. I wasn't up to presidents.

"Miss Francis," he said, "have you ever tasted Lydia Pinkham's Vegetable Compound?"

"No, thank you, sir," I replied, "I mean I'm sure it must be marvelous, but no, I haven't tasted it."

"Well then, do so," he replied, his voice none too friendly.

I might have weaseled out of it and promised to do so as soon as I got home, except for the fact that he had a bottle and a spoon on his desk while he was talking to me.

I began to stumble over words. "Well, I'm not the right *age*—I mean I think it would be . . ." I don't know what I thought it would do if I tasted it, probably make me the mother of four beautiful children and the life of the party, but in any case I was determined to avoid letting a drop pass my lips if it were humanly possible. He was just as determined as I, obviously, and he pointed out that it was my duty to taste it, and to me that translated as "or else." In the end, hanging onto my job was more important than the risk of premature motherhood, so under his watchful eye I took a spoonful, which he had lovingly ladled out. "Why, it's very nice," I said, and he leaned back, nodding with satisfaction.

"The reason I wanted you to do that is because you are very young and just starting out, and there's something you ought to know. Never talk about anything unless you know what you're talking about, and can accurately describe something from experience. You'll be twice as effective if you remember that." (That's not such a bad rule for living, come to think of it.)

Mr. Pinkham's words have had a few side-effects on my personality. It's true they made me a much better saleswoman than I might otherwise have been, but they also turned me into the world's prize customer. It develops that I am something which used to be called a sucker for a pitch, even if I am the one who is making the pitch. "Home" had over forty sponsors, and I tried everything, did everything, ate everything and usually bought everything they offered. I am the proverbial Eskimo to whom they can sell ice-boxes, only the "they" in this case is I.

The prime example of my enthusiasms is the house which Martin and I built in Mount Kisco, New York. The "Home" show commissioned an outstanding architect to design a set of house plans which would incorporate all the latest developments in home conveniences, layout of rooms, heating, flooring, windows, laundry, fabrics, kitchen equipment, whatever goes into building a house. We talked about these things for months on "Home," and before we knew it, Martin and I were sitting in the middle of those plans, and he was bitterly commenting that he was glad "Home" hadn't taken up the architecture of the Taj Mahal as a spring project.

The house we built was adjacent (as those things go in the country, which meant a few acres away) to Bennett and Phyllis Cerf's house, and Phyllis and I laid the carpet ourselves, square by square, with some of the "Home" elves jumping on it to guarantee the adhesion. Needless to say, this carpet was one of the products featured on "Home." As was the do-it-yourself antiquing kit with which I antiqued some chests (and after all this time we still have them and they still look as though I antiqued them—only more so!). If I sold it, I was sold *on* it, and even wholesale it can get pretty expensive if you insist on buying everything you sell.

Of all the shows I ever did, "Home" had the most monumental advance publicity and the most extensive press coverage and reviews after it had been launched. A lot of the coverage was probably due to the innovative nature of the set from which it was telecast, with special emphasis on the cost. Two hundred thousand dollars was the figure mentioned, and if that doesn't sound outrageous, remember that this was 1954. In these inflationary times, the set built for "Home" would cost more like two million dollars.

It was round and divided into segments like the wedges of

a pie, each of which housed one of the regular features of our electronic magazine. We weren't simply a cook-and-sew show, although these skills were included as departments, as they naturally would be in a show aimed at women. (Men weren't doing too much embroidery in the 50s!) We had in addition current events, gardening, family affairs, health, decorating, fashion and beauty. And the "editors" of these various departments were renowned experts in their fields. Dr. Leona Baumgartner, the Commissioner of Health for New York City was in charge of health; Dr. Rose Franzblau, the famous psychologist, was in charge of Family Affairs; Sydney Smith, a beautiful lady in spite of that name, was our decorating expert; Eve Hunter was in charge of fashion and beauty; Poppy Cannon was in charge of food; Will Peigelbeck was our gardening expert; and Estelle Parsons (now an important actress) was our roving reporter. It all called for terrific coordinating talent and fortunately we had that in the person of Phyllis Adams (now Jenkins), who researched, put everything together, wrote, and generally kept us all on the track. In addition, we brought in specialists in all fields, provocative, knowledgeable people for occasional spots, and I think we gave our audience one terrific show every day, Monday through Friday, from 11 A.M. to 12 noon, Eastern time!

"Home" was the first show to employ something called a "monkey camera," which was suspended from above and revolved in order to get into any segment of the set. Jack O'Brian, in reviewing the show in his column, commented, "Be it ever so gadgety, there's no show like 'Home'!" It's absolutely true that we had gimmicks which picked things up, turned them around, lit them and put them away, and all these things generated an excitement of their own, for most of them had never been seen before. There was even one segment of the pie in which we could produce the elements— rain, snow, fog, heat and so on, which we used to demonstrate how certain materials stood up under certain weather conditions.

We may have gone a little hog-wild there at first, pressing buttons and making lights flash with all these shiny toys, like a bunch of kids with a new set of electric trains, but we settled down in short order to letting *people,* rather than gadgets, dominate the show. Hugh Downs, our announcer, was bright and capable, and all the other people I mentioned ran their departments with dispatch. There have been "magazine-type" shows since then, but in my opinion "Home" was the best of the lot, and also in my opinion the reason it isn't still there was because it was *too* good, in a way. It cost so very much to maintain at the high level on which it had started, it simply couldn't survive unless it could be all commercials and no show (that was theoretically possible, by the way, because we couldn't accommodate all the requests we had to buy time on the show).

Since "Home" was live, it naturally opened unparalleled opportunities for my slip-of-the-tongue syndrome to blossom and flourish. (Others were guilty too, but I remember my own gaffes best.) For example, I distinguished myself on our very first show, which had been intended to be introductory. I was to go from department to department, introducing the different editors and chatting about the subjects they would cover on future shows.

When we came to the cooking department, I introduced Poppy Cannon, the well-known nutritionist and a superb cook, and the camera showed the kitchen and the utensils with which she would be working. We had decided that Poppy would do a simple demonstration on this initial show, how to make vichyssoise, and I led off with an introductory remark— "So often we are put off by the French names of various dishes, imagining that they will be very complicated and exotic . . ." I went on to talk about the origins of the lowly potato, how it had come to this country, and how, naturally, it was one of the ingredients we would be working with in our demonstration. "Vichyssoise," I said, "is basically very simple to make." And then, picking up a vegetable from the table, I continued, "First, you take a leek."

What can I tell you? The monkey camera fortunately did not pick up the crew or the dozens of directors and script and production people who fell on the floor laughing, thumping each other on the back, holding their sides and so on, and your fair heroine, what was *she* doing? Absolutely nothing. Just going along as if nothing had been said, because I knew from bitter experience that gasping or apologizing could only compound the felony. I hadn't forgotten that on "What's My Line?" I had once inadvertently said, "Oh my God," a no-no at the time, and then said, "Oh my God, I didn't mean to say 'Oh My God!'"

And then there was the time when I was demonstrating a

knitting machine on "Home." I wore an outfit for the occasion with a top which had been made by the machine, and a skirt which had been knitted by hand. I said, "I just want to show you how hard it is to tell the difference. Will the camera come in close and pan over my body? Thank you. Now then, you are looking at a machine-made top. And this," I continued as the camera eye moved down, "is a hand-made bottom." My magazine of the air became unhinged, but I managed to keep a straight face.

The entire cast and crew had a shot at keeping a straight face during a show which had to do with the Jewish holiday Passover. Our guest was a rabbi who was to describe the foods eaten on that occasion and the religious symbolism connected with it, and we had a Passover seder laid out on a table. The rabbi and I went around the table doing our thing, and when it was over the camera was supposed to lose us and pick up another department. Fine, except for the fact that the rabbi was so intrigued with the electronic devices that he started wandering around on his own, and he meandered into the book section, which as luck would have it, was also where the camera had gone.

"Str-i-ik-e the rabbi!" rang out loud and clear through the studio and through the open microphones for the entire nation to hear—"Goddam strike the goddam rabbi!" It was the voice of the director in the control room, who didn't know his key was open. He was not trying to initiate a pogrom—he was simply trying to get the rabbi out of range of the camera and he got a bit agitated. We all gulped and kept our faces averted and swallowed our laughter while the poor rabbi scurried off the set. Then we sat back and waited for the indignant mail from the Anti-Defamation League to pour in, but it never did. They must have had some members in TV who understood camera terminology.

Fascinating though the physical set of "Home" was, we couldn't do all our shows from there because of our lively current-events segment. We were the first to do what are called "remotes," taking "Home" to wherever there was some exciting action, and that included travelling as far as Japan, in addition to going everywhere in the United States.

On these remotes, we had to bring with us literally tons of equipment, and we had to cope with natural rather than electronic pitfalls. The weather, for example, for a good deal of shooting was done outdoors. Other natural hazards included human beings, chief among whom was a delightful fellow, a writer on the show named Jack Fuller, an imp of a man to whom we were all devoted. Well, perhaps not *all*. Our executive producer had some reservations, such as that he considered Jack to be irresponsible, irreverent, irrelevant, impossible and a maniac, for starters. All of which, by the way, may well have been true, but he was in addition a gifted writer and a barrel of laughs. Our senior producer (not to be confused with the *executive* producer) was named Al Morgan, and he, fortunately for the rest of us, dug Jack's sense of humor, so he protected him, lied for him, and hid him out periodically when the orders would come down to fire him. When the heat had died down, Jack would be back on the job and life was once again unpredictable.

I remember a remote featuring the Army-Navy football game. Glenn Davis, freshly returned from the Korean War, was to be the focus of a sentimental spot—a lone figure in an empty stadium, perhaps, reminiscing about bygone days, evoking the ghosts of former greats who had perished defending freedom in faraway Asia, and Jack was assigned to write it. The assignment was accompanied by dire threats, and Jack promised on his honor to be a good boy. When he had written the spot, he refused to show it to anyone: "No," he said, "I want you to get the full impact. It's the best thing I've ever written, I swear it, but it has to be seen. If you read it on paper it will spoil it." Like idiots, we believed him.

They started the introductory music—"Taps," what else?—and the camera zeroed in on two figures seated alone in the grandstand, dressed in porkpie hats and raccoon coats, standard equipment for the campus set of the twenties. The other piece of standard equipment they had was a hip flask, from which they were swilling as the camera closed in on them. They stood up, fell down and rolled down 125 steps, while we stood around open-mouthed and Jack laughed himself sick. They didn't get hurt, because they were acrobats he had hired, and fortunately it was only a rehearsal—but it cost the producers a potful of money in time consumed, and it goes without saying that Jack was fired once again.

No amount of preparation was too great for a practical

joke where Jack was concerned. In Miami, we did a remote from a hotel where the chef, Philippe, was quite famous. A banquet was given in my honor, and the manager said to me, "Miss Francis, the only thing hotels in this area can compete with is the food we serve. If you could bring yourself to say what a great chef we have, we would appreciate it." I said I'd be happy to oblige, because he *was* wonderful.

Good as my word, as soon as I'd downed the last morsel of *mousse au chocolat avec beaucoup des calories,* I rose, looked appreciatively towards the kitchen and asked if the chef could come out and take a bow. The doors swung open, and a stunned Miss Francis stood there as a caricature Gallic chef with flourishing fake moustache and two-foot-tall white chef's hat minced toward me—Fuller, of course, who'd set the whole thing up. The audience applauded as he took my hand and kissed it all the way up to my shoulder, routed his way around my neck and down the other arm, kissed his fingertips to the audience shouting "Voilà!" and danced back into the kitchen. It took a while for me to recover sufficiently to explain to the dinner guests who he was. They probably had thought this was par for the course for French chefs.

We did one show on "Home" which Al Morgan (who teaches television production) trots out and shows to students every year as a prime example of the maxim: "If anything can go wrong, it will." For once, my part in the general goof-up was minimal. The show was built around the annual fair in Kutztown, Pennsylvania, which is just down the road from Intercourse, Pennsylvania, if anyone cares, in the heart of Pennsylvania Dutch country, so when we announced that the show would be done, there was naturally a lot of quaint talk about shoofly pie and apple pan-dowdy and so on.

My car had broken down on the way there, so that was goof number one. I arrived a trifle late, and it wasn't hard to see that the production staff was a little shaken, because a re-mote is always a cliff hanger, and all it needed was to have the M.C. missing in action. They were relieved when I arrived, but it was too late to brief me on the general format and the director and writer had to fill me in as we went from segment to segment.

One idea we had originally talked about involved country fair music and dancing and merry villagers cavorting about.

This had been knocked into a cocked hat, I learned, because the Amish colony we were visiting forbids music and dance. A leaden hour of people gorging themselves with the aforementioned shoofly pie loomed as a distinct possibility, to our horror, and we were desperate. "What *isn't* forbidden?" we asked the Elders, and they said, "We like story tellers. We have people who are very skilled in telling the old tales." Better than nothing, we thought, and asked them to get us their best.

We sat him in the center of a wide-eyed group and turned the cameras on him. We couldn't understand Pennsylvania Dutch in any case, but obviously the fairgoers loved him, because they were laughing up a storm, which gave us some colorful camera shots. Until, that is to say, a crew member who *did* understand German and a smattering of Pennsylvania Dutch, and could make out what the story was about, came rushing to us, pale as a ghost. "Listen," he said, "this gent is telling a real toilet story, very foul, and we could be in big trouble." I remember thinking, they object to *dancing* as an obscene pastime, but this is okay? Anyway, NBC couldn't afford to take any chances, so we cut him off the air and frantically signaled to Hugh Downs to take over and fill in as best he could.

We were playing in a great open space, and Hugh had to get from one end of a huge field to another to get within camera range. In his mad dash, he tripped over one of the many cables we had all over the place. That was how it happened that instead of a scatological joke in Pennsylvania Dutch, which only a tiny percent of our audience would be likely to understand, the voice of Hugh Downs rang through the land, booming out loud and clear, *"Get that blankety-blank cable out of the way!"*

And judging from the mail, just about everybody understood *that*.

We used to get a large volume of mail which commented on how easy and relaxed we all seemed on the "Home" show, how natural it all looked. This never failed to amuse us, because the "natural look" was the result of the most complicated concentration and planning, and especially in the case of remotes, about seven hours of rehearsal per show. Five days a week. Week-ends off for blood transfusions. But with all the rehearsal in the world, there was no way to guard against the hysterical mishaps which were a guaranteed certainty on remotes.

For instance, we were doing one from the side of the pool at the Beverly Hilton Hotel, which was to feature Olympic divers. Because of the difference in time, we had to get up at 4 A.M. and be out at the pool by 5 A.M. to get things rolling, and begging the Chamber of Commerce's pardon, it was pretty cold and miserable at that hour in California, and we were all looking at each other through a wet blanket of smog, and talking to each other through chattering teeth. By "we" I mean the small army it took to get the show on the tube.

This particular morning, the stage manager was standing at the far side of the pool, away from the diving board, behind him were the vehicles which held all the mechanical equipment. There were cameras all around the pool, and I was standing, waiting at the side. He signalled a young woman wrapped in a horse blanket, calling to her through a megaphone, "All right miss, up on the board! We're ready for your dive!" She discarded her blanket, climbed up and dove. When she surfaced, the stage manager said, "You've got to have a better dive than that! Try it again!" Obediently she climbed the ladder again and took another dive. "Okay," he said, when she came up, "swim over to Arlene," and I beckoned her to where I was standing.

I consulted my list, kneeled at the side of the pool and murmured, "you must be Muriel Crane, the first Olympic diver," into her little blue face.

"N-n-n-no, I'm not," she replied through her clicking teeth.

"Oh?" I said frowning down at the list. "Then you must be Dorothy Janek, the second Olympic diver."

"No. N-n-n-no, I'm not."

Thoroughly bewildered, I said, "Oh? Which diver *are* you?"

"I'm n-n-n-nobody. I'm just a g-g-guest at the hotel."

Now why would anyone in her right mind go through all of that? Just to be a nice kid, is why. She thought they wanted a picture of guests having a good time at the hotel, and she was willing to oblige!

■

Around that time, on our *own* home front, Martin and I were being dispossessed. We had an apartment which we both loved, over at 375 Park Avenue, and were notified that Seagram's had bought the property, were going to tear down the house we lived in and put up their own office building. We were desolate, and even now I find it hard to enjoy the superb cuisine at the Four Seasons Restaurant in the Seagram Building without reflecting that it used to be my dining room. Well, maybe not quite, but in that vicinity.

By a coincidence, I learned that they were planning to toss us out on the street the very same day that I was scheduled to address the liquor industry on behalf of the Cerebral Palsy Foundation, an organization for which I have always worked, and to which the liquor industry has been a very generous contributor. In my speech I said, "To tell the truth, I don't feel terribly friendly about you liquor people at this moment, because I found out today that Seagram's is going to tear down the roof over my head, and all I can say is that I intend to stay right in my bathtub and not move. They'll have to carry me out and set me down in the middle of Park Avenue!"

Seagram's seemed unimpressed with my plight, and the result was that Martin and I went house shopping and found the place I have described, where Judy Garland bewitched us that night. It was an "A" neighborhood and a lovely house, and as these were the 1950s, it cost us $48,000, which, for prime real estate in New York City in *this* year of Our Lord would be considered a gift. To tell you how much of a gift, when we sold the house three years after we'd bought it, and had invested a lot of money rewiring, air-conditioning, new kitchens and so on, we got $85,000—*but* the people to whom we sold it, sold it *one* year later to Loew's, who wanted to build a theater next door, for $250,000. What it would fetch now I refuse to dwell on!

Once again Martin was a monument of self-control in the face of my manic nesting instinct. As with our Mount Kisco house, the town house was filled top to bottom with crates of "Home" sponsors' products. Martin claims that every time he came home, we were having a new kitchen installed, and I hate to admit it but it's almost true. In fact, I had a letter quite recently from a man who had helped install the stove in one of those kitchens—a built-in oven type, so that one wouldn't have to bend over to see what's cooking. He asked if I remembered that Martin had come home while he was there, and I had called out to him, "Mr. Miskit is here to give me a high caloric!"

One of our accounts was Westinghouse, so we had a complete Westinghouse kitchen initially. Then about six months later Westinghouse went somewhere else and we got, I think it was Amana, so out went the Westinghouse and in came Amana. Then General Electric signed on to "Home," and, well, that's the way it went. My little speech to the liquor industry when we were dispossessed brought us some fringe benefits, because they sent over enough spirits of every known description to keep us and all our friends high and happy for some time.

The liquor outlasted our tenure in the house for, as I have said, we had it for only three years. We had to give it up during the period when our royal retainers, Nicholas and Alexandra, were in residence, and they occupied a room at the top of the house. Peter's room was just under theirs, and ours was under his.

It was during the summer, and I was playing in Robert Sherwood's play, *The Road to Rome,* up in Westport, Connecticut, in stock. Martin had driven up to fetch me home. We got back into the city at about 1:30 A.M. and saw from the street that the house was ablaze with light. We dashed in to find Nicholas and Alexandra being very emotionally Russian as they were being questioned by a policeman, and a wide-awake, very excited Peter jumping up and down. Thieves had broken in, had apparently known exactly which room was ours, and had burgled it in leisurely fashion while Nicholas, Alexandra and Peter slept on, blissfully unaware of what was happening. When the thieves left, they hadn't bothered to turn off the lights or close the door, and a suspicious neighbor had sent for the police.

Once again I was jewelry-less, except for the diamond heart and my wedding ring, which I always wore. The jewelry wasn't the Hope Diamond or anything in the Elizabeth Taylor tradition, but it isn't the intrinsic value I'm talking about. Being robbed does something worse than deprive you of possessions—it robs you of your sense of privacy. The feeling of being violated is terribly strong, for the general pattern of housebreakers is that they are not only thieves, they are vandals who derive pleasure, I believe, from creating a sense of destruction. Cigarettes were ground into the carpet, things taken out of drawers and off walls and flung around the room, as though the thieves were making a contemptuous comment. It is something indescribable. Nothing material we lost was as important as our sense of security, and we sadly concluded, as we put our charming house on the market, that without that, a house is not a home.

14

Everybody has despairing moments, I suppose, and they would include everything from getting a run in your stocking to being hijacked. I have them too, of course, and to overcome them, I have only to remember the rewarding experiences I had when I was working on "Home"—among them an hour-long program about and with Helen Keller. Who could feel sorry for herself, thinking about that incredible lady?

It seems to me that Helen Keller was somebody we learned about in school, somebody who had already become a legend when I was a child. (I'm not sure I didn't think she was somebody the book writers had made up for the benefit of gullible children who needed to be taught to count their blessings.) "Legend" is one of those words that gets tossed around like "superstar" nowadays, to describe things a few degrees above mediocre, so I wish I could think of a better word to attach to Helen Keller. All I can say is that meeting her was an immensely emotional happening for me, and that it is the recollection of that meeting and of her inspirational life which brings me to heel and makes anything unfortunate that could happen to me seem insignificant.

Although I knew better, at the outset of the show I spoke very slowly and distinctly, feeling that she could lip-read and I would make it easier for her. I simply wasn't able to take in that she was blind, for her face was so animated, so responsive that even her eyes seemed to follow you. The reason for that, of course, was that as I talked, her companion, teacher—her "eyes and ears"—Polly Thompson, described what was happening in the studio in Miss Keller's palm, and she put her fingers gently to my lips as I spoke. By the movement and vibrations of my lips, she knew what I was saying, so she really could lip-read in a way. I was so affected by all of this, I could hardly keep the tears out of my eyes—but they weren't tears of sadness, goodness knows, they were tears of wonder at what the human spirit is capable of accomplishing.

We "talked" about her long career, about how she had appeared all over the world, about her start with her first teacher, the remarkable Annie Sullivan, whose dedication and determination had wrought the original miracle which had made Helen Keller the beacon for every person in the world to look to. Not just those who are physically handicapped, but all of us who need to be reminded from time to time of Shakespeare's immortal phrase, "What a work of God is man!" Because of Helen Keller's achievement, we are *all* ennobled.

On the "Home" show, we often had people as guests who represented that same spirit to me, the affirmation of life. We aimed very high in our search for such guests, and it wasn't always easy to get them. Carl Sandburg, for example. It took a lot of guile to persuade him to appear, because he was on record as having publicly stated his implacable animosity toward our medium. What is more, the forum upon which he had voiced his sentiments was a symposium in which we *both* had participated.

I'd gone down to Asheville, North Carolina, for a convention of the General Federation of Women's Clubs, and Mr. Sandburg and I were appearing the same evening. I was to follow him as a speaker, so imagine my dismay when, listening with rapt attention to one of my life-long heroes, I heard him blasting everything I was connected with—TV, radio, the movies—saying such endearing things as "Commercial shows are filled with inanities, assininities, silliness and cheap trickery."

Of *course* there are programs which fit that description, but there are others too, and I found myself getting defensive and saying, "He doesn't have to listen, he can always turn it off . . . ," but Mr. Sandburg had no intention of being turned off *himself*. He continued about movies, talking about a lad he knew who went to the movies about thirty times a year. "Even if he went only once a month it would be too much," he said, "because *that* silly industry doesn't *make* twelve good pictures a year!"

As for his fellow poets, there was none of that spurious professional courtesy when he talked about *them* either, I can tell you! He claimed, in fact, that the only poetry that got printed in these ridiculous times was "symbolic," and that if a line meant what it said, it didn't stand a chance. He was the old curmudgeon down to his fingertips, and I was bemused, amused and riled all at the same time. (When he was asked later, after the symposium, whether he and I were still friends, he said, "Why of course, we're old college chums!")

As he had done his level best to put an end to everything at which I earned a living, I thought it no more than fair that I try to get even with him. I challenged him before witnesses to come on the "Home" show, promising that he would be allowed to speak his piece, to say whatever he pleased and, to my vast surprise, he accepted.

I was girded for battle, but there's no point in beating around the bush. Almost from the moment we were on camera, I was defeated, for I fell madly in love with this silver-haired, ascetic-faced, brilliant wit. He looked as though he'd been dreamed up by Norman Rockwell for the cover of the *Saturday Evening Post,* the perfect prototype of a homespun American, sitting on a cracker barrel, fascinating the locals with his chatter. He fascinated A. Francis with no trouble at all with his pungent comments about everyone and everything, and I had to keep reminding myself that he was old enough to be my father, for he was younger in spirit than anyone I'd ever met.

He wasn't *merely* acid! He was surprisingly gentle about a number of things—including the goats which he and his wife raised on the plantation where we were filming the program. He introduced me to the goats, all of which had fanciful names such as Brocade and Silver, and insisted that goats were among the most misunderstood and maligned of animals. "Why," he said in mock indignation, "it's a rank canard that they eat tin cans! They wouldn't dream of such a thing unless they were filled with caviar!" He coaxed me into tasting some ice cream which Mrs. Sandburg had made from goat's milk, and I pretended it was the greatest treat I'd ever had. For all I can remember about the taste, I might actually have thought it *was,* because I had reached a state where I was prepared to believe anything Carl Sandburg wanted me to! He got out his guitar and sang to me, told me about his life, about the books he'd written about Lincoln, and about *Remembrance Rock,* meandering in and out of bypaths in his life so that I felt I'd known him forever.

He was so *simpatico* that I was emboldened to mention the book I'd been persuaded to write on the subject of charm, *That Certain Something,* and he courteously asked me to send him a copy. I don't know how I had the nerve to comply, but I did send it—as though Carl Sandburg needed me to tell him about charm—and he wrote me a letter which is one of my treasures. In it he told me that I had an Emersonian style, and that we could have a wonderful life, reading each other's books! Now that's what *I* call charm!

There are countless stories in my scrapbook, countless pictures of the "Home" years, of us flying everywhere to cover this festival, that fair, but if I had to pick *one,* I suppose the most exotic remote we were ever invited to do was in Japan.

The Japanese government had issued the invitation, and we considered it a great honor that of all the shows on the air, they were most interested in ours. The war had ended about ten years earlier, and the Japanese were employing every speck of their considerable ingenuity in rebuilding their country, as well as rebuilding their ties to the West, most especially to the United States. I believe they saw "Home" as the most down-to-earth way of introducing the Japanese and the customs of Japan to an American audience, and if their object was to impress the personnel involved in the "Home" show favorably, so that we would be friendly in telling their story, they succeeded admirably.

Miss Francis in kimono, Miss Francis eating sukiyaki with a Japanese family in their home, Miss Francis being given a lesson in flower-arrangement and learning about the tea ceremony, Miss Francis beside herself with delight in Osaka at the Bunraku puppet show, Miss Francis with geisha trainees in Kyoto, Miss Francis backstage at Kabuki—all these scenes and pictures are things which one would expect to see on the program (programs, for we were there for ten days), and indeed all of these came to pass. But there were unexpected things too, for Japan continued to unfold to us with surprises, and as we learned about them, we showed them to our audience.

We happened to be in Tokyo on New Year's Eve, for example, and I had imagined a saki-inspired typical celebration such as I was accustomed to at home. I was totally unprepared for the reality—mile-long processions to every shrine, quiet, orderly, beautiful. I was filled with admiration for the spiritual quality of an entire nation going to the shrine to pray for the New Year and to pay their respects to their ancestors, instead of what I was used to—an entire nation going out on the town and getting loaded!

One thing that happened to me during the Japanese remote had nothing to do with the show. It was an unexpected visitor to my room at the old Imperial Hotel, which had been built by Frank Lloyd Wright. Early one morning there was a knock at my door. I opened it to a very old, wrinkled Japanese gentleman, who stood bowing and smiling and chattering away as though he expected me to know every word he uttered.

"Wrong place, wrong place!" I said very loud, as one has a tendency to do when speaking to someone in a language she doesn't understand—as though sheer volume will make the alien words intelligible.

As I was about to close the door, I heard two words which sounded familiar—"Joshua Rogan."

Now, Joshua Logan is hardly a name you expect to have hurled at you at 7:30 A.M. in Tokyo, but suddenly I remembered and shouted "Of *course!* You're the pearl man!" Josh had been to Japan and had told me about somebody who would give me a very good price on pearls, and he had followed up his suggestion by writing to the man and telling him to call on me.

The pearl bearer opened case after case and spread them around the dresser, my bed, on the floor, and eventually some wound up around my neck because I did buy some. (I've always meant to ask Josh what *he* means by cheap. These certainly came from very pampered oysters.) At any rate, the pearl man mentioned *en passant* that he might make a trip to the U.S.A. and where could he find me? (He obviously recognized lack of sales resistance when he saw it.) I muttered something about working in Rockefeller Center, and he beamed. "Ah soo! Mr. Rockeferrer very good friend, arways buy pearls from me!" From his point of view, now we had two friends in common, Joshua Logan and Nelson Rockefeller, and a girl with friends like that couldn't be a bargain hunter, could she? Maybe that's why my pearls were so costly.

I loved my visit to Japan, my look at a culture which was so strange to me. I understand that many traditions are fading to make way for the industry which has brought Japan to such prosperous heights, and I'm sorry about that in a sentimental way, but I suppose it is inevitable. I think the Japanese enjoyed us as much as we did them, and I even got a thank-you letter from the then Prime Minister, Ichiro Hatoyama, for coming. The letter talked about developing understanding, and said, "Through the medium of programs like yours, mutual understanding and trust between the Nations of the Earth [his capitals] are achieved. I hope you will extend the greetings of the Japanese people as well as mine to the splendid women of America." All right, all you splendid women, I'm a little late, but here you are.

I think everyone who has ever conducted an interview program on radio or television will agree that just as important as knowing how to talk, is knowing how *not* to talk. If you are a talker by nature, as I am, shutting up is something you actually have to *learn,* and it takes a certain amount of self discipline. The bright rejoinder, the witty riposte (or to put it another way, the smart-aleck wisecrack) does not always enhance your program. It can, in fact, kill it dead by interrupting the flow of your guest's thought.

It was on "What's My Line?" that I learned the most about listening. I made the discovery that by paying attention to the questions my fellow panelists put and to the answers given by the guest, I could learn a lot more than by concentrating on what *my* next question would be. The listening habit grew stronger on the "Home" show, and it is the very essence of my WOR radio program, which I have been doing for seventeen years. What it boils down to is that when one's guests are fascinating people—and why else would one invite them to come on a program and talk about themselves?—it behooves you to let them do the entertaining if they are at all capable of it.

(All of which is, of course, a gross over-simplification. I will not deny that certain interviewers feel quite differently about this, and have had very successful, if controversial, programs using abrasive third-degree questioning techniques. It happens not to be my bag for I feel that if an interviewer does all the talking, he is using a guest only as a sounding board for his own opinions, and in fact I shrink from even listening to a guest being what I consider to be abused. But that's strictly personal.)

If the guest is to come off well, the interviewer must do a lot of homework. The book must be read, the play must be seen, the career must be studied. Somehow or other the interviewer must try to get some insights about the guests, for even the author of a gory book or grand guignol play may be the shyest, most retiring of creatures. Or the guest might have a terrible case of stage fright at the sight of a microphone or camera, or have a rambling, discursive way of talking. Time is the villain on every ad-lib show, and to keep the program moving along at a lively pace, the host must know exactly what questions to ask so that even the most reticent guest can relax and know he won't be left floundering on his own. To know those questions takes hours and hours of preparation for every program, and as far as I am concerned, all that study has done me a lot more good than Finch Finishing School ever did, and has given me a college education I couldn't have bettered behind ivied walls.

The most serious pitfall is the danger of trying to outshine your guest. As an example, wouldn't it have been foolish to do anything but *listen* as I sat on a park bench in the Boston Commons with Joseph Welch. We did an hour-long program with that magnificent lawyer (later judge) just after he had reminded America of the meaning of honor and decency during the infamous McCarthy–Army hearings, and he spoke with warmth and humor of his life and philosophy.

Maybe I have a thing for rural-type sages for, as with Carl Sandburg, by the time the hour was over, I felt Joseph Welch had been a life-long friend. Also as with Sandburg, he sent me a letter confirming our *rapport*. It said, in part: "Well by gosh, no one is ever going to name a rose after *me*." (There is an Arlene Francis rose. Doesn't look a bit like me.) "Possibly some new vegetable, such as a cross between a head of cabbage and a rutabaga, but I bet I'll miss even that. My moments spent with you on the park bench remain with me quite a shining memory, and with my friends and relatives too!" Judge Welch doesn't need anything named after him to remind us all how deeply we are in his debt for helping us redeem our dignity.

(Small digression: If this had happened a few years later, Judge Welch could have mentioned my other namesake, a horse named Arlene Francis.

Some years ago Drew Dudley introduced me to Mrs. William Woodward, to whom columnists refer as "the doyenne of New York society"; but in the hearts of those lucky enough to know her, she is one of the most beloved, remarkable women of our time. Elsie Woodward has weathered every storm with her patrician head held high, and today into her nineties her interests are so catholic that she is more pleasure to be with than many of my contemporaries.

Elsie and her husband William Woodward bred horses on their Belaire Farms, and one morning she called me. "Arlene," she said, "we have a new foal, a full sister of Damascus, and I wondered if you would object to our naming her Arlene Francis?"

Object! Well, I couldn't have been more flattered. Not many of us could boast an ancestry like that of Damascus: by Sword Dancer out of Karela by My Babu! Damascus was considered one of the best horses of the century, winning the Preakness and the Belmont Stakes in 1967. Yes, right, I'm showing off. It's Martin who knows statistics like that.

At any rate, I accepted the honor Mrs. Woodward was conferring on me with pleasure, and could hardly wait until Arlene [she doesn't mind my calling her by her first name] was at the track.

The day of her maiden race, I was exactly like a nervous mother, asking myself, "What if she doesn't do well?" and I asked Elsie if I oughtn't to put a small bet down just to encourage her. "Oh no, my dear," she said, "not yet. We're simply trying her out to see how she gets on with the other horses in this one."

I couldn't go to the race in any case, because I was working in a TV show, but I dashed to the phone when the race was over to see how she'd done. When I got the news that Arlene Francis had won her first race, I could hardly be contained. All around the studio I spread the news—"She win! she win!" in good race-trackese.

Arlene has had a distinguished, if not spectacular record

and is, as of this writing, in foal—and I don't in the least mind becoming a grand-godmother to a horse.)

"Home" was on NBC over twenty years ago, and my memories of it are so vivid because it enriched every day of my life. There was one day, for example, when "Home" went to Washington and visited, among others, the junior Senator from Massachusetts John Fitzgerald Kennedy and his beautiful wife, Jacqueline. She met the crew at the door with a trayful of martinis, for she knew we had been earlier to the home of a rather stiff-necked Republican. "Here," she said, "you probably need these! I understand you've been trapped with Republicans!" We took them gratefully, but what I mostly remember was a feeling of great purposefulness on the part of the Senator, and of reticence on the part of the dark-eyed Jackie. She was genuinely shy, and it was no affectation—but Senator Kennedy was so outgoing and winning, so articulately witty, that at dinner that night, back in New York, I said to Martin, "You know what? The junior Senator from Massachusetts wants to be President of the United States, and it wouldn't surprise me in the least if he makes it."

I had the same feeling when the Governor of Georgia was a guest on "What's My Line?" He was unknown to all of us at the time, but he took not being recognized with amazing good humor and was enchanting with all of us after the show. He followed it up with a letter inviting me to come to Atlanta, saying that he and Rosalynn would be so pleased to have me at the Governor's Mansion. It was a "y'all come, hear?" sort of folksiness, and though I never went, I strongly felt that Jimmy Carter had national ambitions and wasn't going to be forgotten. I wonder if he'll repeat the invitation from his new address.

There were all sorts of dynamic people to listen to and to learn from, and it strikes me that some may wonder why anyone of the stature of, say Dr. William Menninger, or Trygve Lie or Carlos Romulus or Mme. Pandit would come on a TV spectacle or a radio talk show. It's simple. They wanted public support for an idea, and the best way to reach the public was through a medium with a vast audience.

"Home" was an educational program, and in pursuit of our goals to inform the public, J. Edgar Hoover made his files available to us when we did a program on kidnapping (and wrote voluble thanks when it was over); I was the first woman in history to ring the bell and pound down the gavel to open the New York Stock Exchange; I went down in a diving bell in California and up on a cat cracker (oil refinery) in Cleveland. As I say, we were an educational program, and the one it educated most of all was me. I mean I.

15

I want to get something off my mind—the fact that I mentioned having written a book about charm. That really isn't as pretentious as it sounds, and it sounds pretty damned pretentious I'll admit. The publisher responsible for the idea replied to my astonished negative reaction by suggesting that I find a *way* to do it; not as a how-to book, but one which would focus on observations about where I had witnessed charm at work. Well, that didn't sound too self-serving or egotistical, and added to that was the fact that the publisher had offered me a stunning advance, publisherese for coin of the realm. I found that extremely charming, and I said yes.

The only thing I want to mention in connection with that book is that I wrote to a number of people asking for a definition of charm, and among them was Mrs. Roosevelt. (As opposed to all the Mrs. Roosevelts who were and are around, she was *the* Mrs. Roosevelt who needs no further identification.)

Instead of telling me to get lost and that she had no time for such nonsense—or ignoring my letter, which was also a possibility—she wrote a gracious reply, saying she'd given the subject much thought and had concluded that the only thing that matters in the relationship between two human beings is kindness, and that she wasn't, therefore, qualified to comment on charm. In writing that, she really summed up everything there was to say about charm, but in spite of that I wrote the book, and that's the last word on *that* subject!

The demise of the "Home" show was a great sadness to me—to all of us connected with it, in fact. To be that frantically busy for four years, and suddenly to find yourself all revved up and hear the race is called off—it's terribly unnerving. It's not really fair to say it was sudden. It's just that we couldn't believe it would actually happen.

We were in Silver Springs, Florida, when we got word that the show was doomed. We were doing a remote, and to the chagrin of the Chamber of Commerce, it had poured steadily ever since we had arrived. Our spirits were damp enough without the news of our cancellation, and Hugh Downs and I sat down and wrote a parody of Rodgers & Hart's "Bewitched, Bothered and Bewildered," which we performed for the cast and crew:

> *We've met again*
> *On the set again*
> *And as you can see we are wet again,*
> *Sick, cancelled and hung over*
> *Are we.*
>
> *We're low again*
> *Have no show again*
> *And what there is of it we'll blow again,*
> *Sick, cancelled and hung over*
> *Are we.*
>
> *Lost our jobs, but what of it*
> *Silver Springs, you've been cricket*
> *NBC you can shove it*
> *And failing that, you can stick it.*
>
> *Renewed we're not*
> *And cued we're not*
> *Monastic and chaste, even screwed we're not,*
> *Sick, cancelled and hung over*
> *Are we.*

One magazine article put it, "NBC has made the most unkindest cut of all," and spoke of "Home" as being the most intelligent and ambitious show on the air. It was both of those things, I think, but sad to say, the networks have always demonstrated that it is not their job to educate the public. If that educational process happens along the way, that's gravy and groovy, but networks are primarily in business for the purpose of making money, and the public itself dictates what it wishes to see. Our public was vociferous, but not big enough to justify the tremendous cost of the show, and so it ended, a victim of the rating game.

After "Home" closed down, NBC tried to find something else for me to do, for they still nurtured warm feelings toward me and wanted to keep me in the fold. While we were discussing what I might do, they brought up a possibility which ranks with the major "if Idas" of my life. Everybody has them. "If Ida done this" or "If Ida done that"—what changes would it have made in my life? Well, if Ida done what NBC suggested—taken over the "Today" show—ah well, I didn't, and if that sounds regretful, I don't mean it to. There was only *one* occasion on which I uttered a rueful "Damn!" and I'll come to that, but for all the rest, I've never been in the least sorry that I said no.

I had often presided over the "Today" show, filling in for Dave Garroway, who was the host at that time, when he was on vacation, just as I'd filled in on the other NBC blockbuster, "Tonight," substituting for Jack Paar from time to time. I had enjoyed doing them both, but I think that was because I didn't have to do them regularly. It was bad enough getting up at four in the morning when we did remotes on "Home," but that and my occasional stint of getting to the studio before dawn for "Today" had made me aware that as a way of life, it wasn't for me. I felt (rightly or wrongly) that it would have caused too great an upheaval in my relationships with family and friends.

I added up the possibilities: on the credit side of the ledger there was a whopping salary, enough to make even *me*, with my built-in fear of poverty, feel secure—probably for the rest of my life. (Provided, as Henny Youngman once said, that I didn't live past four o'clock today. Inflation wasn't an issue at that time.) And another temptation—a tremendous one when you are offered a challenge of that nature, is to prove that you *can* handle it. However, the debit side of the ledger outweighed both those considerations: a curtailment of my family life, an end to my social life, and farewell forever to any hope of doing plays on Broadway.

I was positive that there were people who could take getting up at that hour every day in their stride, but I simply couldn't see myself doing it. I *could* see myself being a pain in the neck to hostesses, watching the clock to make sure I got home and was in bed by 10 P.M. with anti-wrinkle cream under my eyes. And I thought about Martin being on his own most evenings—what sort of life would that be for him? (Maybe marvelous, which would make it even worse!) Thus, although I had always been accustomed to talking such career decisions over with Martin, this was the time I decided to make my decision independent of his advice. I was afraid that in his desire not to stand in the way, he might try to be "gallant" and persuade me to do something he didn't want me to do.

And so, when Dave Tebet and some other NBC executives came to see me and formally offered me "Today" with Hugh Downs as co-host, I heard them out and flatly said no. Not *let me think it over* or *I'd like to sleep on this.* Just no, n-o, no. (And, of course, thank you.)

And by the way, to set the record straight—even if I hadn't had such overwhelming personal reasons for not wanting to do "Today," I would certainly have balked at the idea of being a "co-host." It was a time during which I was riding the crest of a wave—guest appearances, Woman of the Year, award shows, and "What's My Line?" Several regular shows were offered me, and all in all I saw no reason why I should be a "co-host"! Well yes, my ego *was* a touch out of hand, and though I loved Hugh Downs and we had worked well together on "Home," I was in that period of my life when I felt I deserved to be top banana. I figured something better would present itself—and I think this should be a warning to the current crop of hot personalities: beware delusions of immortality!

NBC did come up with something for me, a show to be called "The Arlene Francis Show," which, if you happen to be Arlene Francis, is a title that's hard to resist. It was to be a potpourri of pure entertainment, a variety show with absolutely no educational overtones, no sirree, no more multi-syllabic words to cut down on the rating. I would preside as M.C. making funnies, ad-libbing with the rest of the talent, sort of Bob Hope with curls. I said fine, it sounded good to me, which goes to show what *I* know.

Meanwhile, back at the executive offices, some bright fellow came up with the thought that a hard-working script girl and occasional writer on "Today" ought to be given a crack at that co-hosting job, so they tried her out and Barbara Walters was launched on one of the most spectacular careers that's ever happened in television. And how did I feel about *that?* I thought and think it was the most marvelous thing that could possibly happen, the very embodiment of the American dream come true. This young woman whom nobody had ever heard of, was being given a chance to shine purely on her own merits, without any fancy reputation behind her and her merits were very bright ones. We have since become good friends, and she knows she has no more sincere admirer than I.

In no way do I wish to imply that I could have done as well as Barbara with that show—it is not one of those things I brood over; brooding isn't my style in any case. But I said earlier that there was an *If Ida* connected with that episode: The only time I felt a twinge of envy about not doing "Today" was many years later, when I read that the show was going to China as part of the entourage of the history-making trip with President Nixon. If Ida said yes to Dave Tebet I'd have gone to China, and how I would have loved that! (If the representatives of the People's Republic of China read these lines and get any ideas from them, I accept!)

There is another *if Ida* in my life which could have changed the course of things for me; it has to do with a musical that I didn't do. Steve Sondheim, the composer-lyricist, and Arthur Laurents, the writer-director, came to see me when I replaced Margaret Leighton in the play *Tchin-Tchin.* The next day they offered me the lead in a new musical they had written called *Anyone Can Whistle.* "I'd *love* to do a musical," I told them, "but I don't sing, I don't dance, and isn't that what you're supposed to do in a musical?" "Pooh," they poohed. I was to look at Rex Harrison. (With pleasure.) All right, did he sing? Did he dance? Was *My Fair Lady* a flop? Very well, what about Roz Russell? Did she sing? Did she dance? Had *Wonderful Town* failed because she couldn't do those things? Or had Walter Huston in *Knickerbocker Holiday* ruined "The September Song" by Kurt Weill because he had no singing voice? That's the kind of logic that can put the theater out of business, but never mind. I was encouraged and I read the script. Unfortunately, I didn't feel it was right for me.

Okay, they said, and found somebody who said it was right for *her*, Angela Lansbury, who had never done a musical either. Now it's true the show was a failure, but the critics adored Angela, and well they might have, for she was enchanting in the role. The result was that producers, directors and so on who saw the show marked her in their minds as a *musical* best bet, and it has certainly turned out that way. *Maybe* if Ida . . . but I didn't.

"The Arlene Francis Show" made it possible for me to look around for a Broadway play to do, as it made few demands on my time. Fortunately I didn't have to look very far. Just across the breakfast table to Martin Gabel, who was about to go into production with a marvelously funny show called *Once More with Feeling*, written by our friend Harry Kurnitz.

For the benefit of those who are now saying to themselves, "Oh *well*, naturally being the producer's wife she'd have no *problem*." I hope you will accept my assurances that the exact opposite is true. Even if Martin thought I would be ideal, he'd be the last to say so! More likely he'd say, "I'm not sure Arlene would be right, but somebody of her general physical type . . ." Nor would Kurnitz be swayed by the fact that we were his closest friends. If he didn't agree with Martin, he'd say, "Arlene? You have to be crazy!" An author's play is as dear to him as his child (more so if he has no children, as in Harry's case) and he takes no chances he doesn't have to take, so when Martin said to me, "Listen Arlene, *Harry* has suggested that you ought to play the part of the wife," I knew Harry hadn't been persuaded because I was sleeping with the producer.

I'd read the play and loved it, and had hoped somebody would think of me, so I leapt across the breakfast table and gave Martin a terrific hug. "I take it," he said, wiping the egg off his shirt, "that means the answer is yes."

Once More with Feeling had a cozy aura. Besides Martin and Harry another old friend, George Axelrod, was the director and Joe Cotten would co-star marking the first time Joe and I would have worked together in many years, since we'd done a daffy Italian comedy called *Horse Eats Hat* at the Mercury Theater, under the aegis of Orson Welles. Joe hadn't done too badly in the intervening years, and now the Hollywood star was coming home, to our joy. In a lesser role was an up-and-coming actor who hadn't quite made it as yet, named Walter Matthau, and we were all crazy about him too—so it was all in the family, theater style.

We were a very big hit, for nobody ever wrote funnier lines or designed wackier farce situations than Harry Kurnitz, but the farce situation I remember best in that play was one Harry didn't write. One scene called for me to race on stage in pajama tops, which were just long enough to cover the subject, as we used to say. On this particular night, my pajama top got caught in the doorway as I entered, and wound up not covering much of anything. As Joe remarked after the performance, "Well Arlene, there's one audience that knows your true colors!"

It should be remembered that this happened before it became a commonplace to see actors and actresses stripped to the buff, and long before anatomy had replaced playwriting as a surefire means of getting a laugh. (Off the burlesque circuit, that is to say.) The audience screamed its delight, and though that is a very seductive, pleasant sound to an actress, I valiantly resisted all suggestions that I leave the scene in for future performances.

Once More with Feeling was one of my happiest theater experiences. (Another was *Tchin-Tchin*, which I have mentioned. That one had special meaning for me because it was a "serious," difficult role, instead of light comedy with which I was usually identified, and it was so well received, it gave me a lovely sense of achievement.)

Busy though I was, there was a nagging suspicion in my mind that the success train I'd been riding for so many years had begun to slow down. "The Arlene Francis Show" had been a disappointment to NBC and to me, and I began to have attacks of self-doubt. Almost every performer has them at one time or another, and they're not a bad thing to have because they keep you from getting smug even when you *are* riding high. This time, however, there was some justification for how I felt. *What has she done lately?* is not an uncommon approach in show business, and what *I* had done lately for NBC was to be the star of two very expensive failures. (Although it isn't fair to call "Home" a failure—a four-year run and tremendous sponsorship is hardly a disaster area.) I wasn't ready for unemployment insurance, but it *did* worry me.

I will admit to being a little neurotic on the subject of impending doom. That is to say, it would be neurotic if I were in a sensible business which had retirement plans and benefits and so on, but show business people are, as a class, the most insecure gypsies on the face of the earth for the very good reason that their principal asset—talent—is so ephemeral. Our point of view is "It can't last," and unfortunately we're right more often than we're wrong.

But in my case, that was only *one* reason I would get depressed if I weren't working every minute. The other was a legacy from my father, whose traumatic experiences as a penniless immigrant had left him badly scarred and had ingrained in me since childhood a tremendous need for security.

That I should have been having such feelings at a time when a newspaper story about me and Martin mentioned our joint income as being rather impressive does indeed sound neurotic. Nor was the figure they mentioned a gross exaggeration—which is to say the *gross* was accurate, but the *net* was something else again. I don't mean to sound like a Wall Street tycoon ranting about taxes, but it *is* true that people in the entertainment world often wind up broke because their salaries, no matter how great, are taxed as straight income. As I said, their principal asset is *talent* and there is no allowance for talent depletion as there would be for, say, oil depletion. In short, Martin's and my take-home pay was less impressive than the published figures, and our expenses were considerable.

One of those expenses had to do with my parents. Although my father had earned a substantial amount as a successful photographer, he had invested it in the stock market, buying on margin as did a great many other people just before 1929. The international insanity that swept up the bedazzled get-rich-quickers engulfed Daddy too—and the disaster which wiped them out did the same to him. It wasn't on the same scale as the paper-billionaires who were throwing themselves out of windows, but Daddy was able to paper his room with telegrams which said, "We need ten thousand dollars by morning to cover your stock," and variations on that theme. He kept them up there to remind himself never again to put money into the stock market.

Fortunately, and I use the word advisedly, he changed his mind about that. When he started to earn some money again, he bought blue-chip stocks which supported him and Mother when he retired. At least they were supposed to, and for a while they served admirably, but life has a funny way of sneaking surprises in on you. Daddy's mistake was not in buying stocks, it was in retiring.

It often happens with people who are mentally and physically capable of carrying on, that retirement turns out *not* to be a blessing. That was precisely what happened to Daddy. He had never learned how to cope with leisure—not in large doses. You have to have a special talent for that, one which you don't develop if you are reared with a "work ethic" philosophy which dictates that it is sinful not to improve each shining hour. Daddy puttered around a bit, not knowing quite what to do with himself, harboring deep feelings of guilt because he was not being "productive," whatever that means. He read a bit, painted a bit, pastimes which he had treasured during his working years, but which now palled when they loomed as his sole occupation. Gradually he became withdrawn—*so* gradually that we didn't notice it particularly until we were forced to look and see that something was amiss.

We couldn't ignore the growing habit of forgetfulness, the wandering of ideas, the onset, in short, of senility. Let me quickly add that everybody—or most everybody—is apt to get a little forgetful as the years pile up. I prefer to think of that as "selective remembrance," when you've lived long enough to decide what you *want* to remember in detail. Daddy's forgetfulness was not like that at all. He had begun to have fantasies of living in another period of his life from time to time, and there were other, alarming episodes. Mother called me in the middle of the night once because Daddy had left his bed and wandered down the corridor outside their apartment in his pajama tops. She hadn't told me until then that for a considerable time, she had practically not slept at all because of his newly acquired habit of sleepwalking. That and his failing physical health had begun to take a terrible toll of her own health.

We consulted a couple of doctors, and the consensus was that Daddy could no longer be looked after by just Mother, that he needed professional, custodial care. As anyone who has ever had to face such a problem will verify, this is among the most difficult decisions in the world to make. Sensible, objective, intelligent judgment dictates one thing, but emotions and yes, one's guilts, have very little to do with being "sensible." We were just about destroyed by our conflicts, but there was no argument with the fact that Mother could not look after him, nor, it goes without saying, could I. We therefore began the difficult, the unbelievably depressing task of looking for what we hoped would be the "right" place for Daddy. We found a comparatively pleasant nursing home in the Riverdale-Fieldston section, where we had once lived.

What recommended this place to me and to Mother was the area itself, the open spaces, the lovely vista that we knew Daddy had loved, and we hoped he would feel as though he were coming home. Indeed, when we brought him there, he seemed perfectly content, but Mother and I made one immense error of judgment which I wish to include here for the benefit of people who might be tempted to make a similar error on the assumption that they are doing a good thing: we insisted that Daddy have his own private room. It would have been far better for him to have a companion, a roommate with whom he could have had some kind of human relationship. Sometimes even an abrasive relationship that keeps the adrenaline flowing is better than being alone, a status which often leads to incurable depression. We didn't know that, and we thought Daddy would prefer his independence.

He was there for a few years, and of course he didn't improve, and though I went up every weekend and Mother went up during the week, I began to feel that it would be better if he were closer to us, so that I could drop in after work every day, and Mother could walk over whenever she pleased. We moved him into another very agreeable, quite pleasant nursing home in the east Sixties, and he was there for another year before he died.

It is a heartbreaker to see someone you love deteriorate before your eyes, and I can remember the pleasure I took from the most minor breaks in Daddy's general depression. As once, when I brought him some picture magazines (he enjoyed looking at them although he could no longer concentrate on the text), among them *Playboy*. Daddy opened the magazine to the centerfold of a nude woman, and like a mischievous boy, he looked up at me with twinkling eyes and winked. I lived on the memory of that wink for weeks.

Martin was pure gold through all of these dreadful years. He was supportive, helpful, and in addition, he was wonderfully gentle with my mother. When Father died, it was as much his idea as mine that Mother should move into the hotel in which we lived. She was bewildered and unhappy, and the fact that we wanted her close to us so that she could have the feeling that she was living with her family, even though not in the same apartment, buoyed her up considerably. It was also easier for me, because I am a chronic worrier about the people I love.

As everyone who has read the papers knows, the cost of nursing homes is an open scandal—even the rotten ones, whose owners are spending time in jail for their ripoffs, cost a fortune. The good ones, such as the ones Daddy was in—well, all I can say is that the publicized amount that Martin and I were supposed to be earning was none too much. And all of this brings me back to square one—my inclination to panic about money when my career seemed to have reached an impasse. Poor Daddy had certainly thought he had prepared for a comfortable old age with those blue-chip dividends. So much for the best-laid plans of mice and men.

Yes, for a minute there, when "The Arlene Francis Show" went off the air, and *Once More with Feeling* had its closing notice posted up on the bulletin board backstage, Pollyanna went out to lunch. Mind, it was often lunch with caviar, as "What's My Line?" was still a powerhouse—but the Glad Girl psychology was wearing a little thin here and there!

16

Billy Wilder, one of Hollywood's more enduring wonder-boys, brought the roses back to my cheeks with the offer of a role in a movie he was going to make called *One, Two, Three.* I was flattered that the great Wilder wanted me to play the part of Jimmy Cagney's wife, considering that my entire motion picture career and experience so far had consisted of the role in *Murders in the Rue Morgue* at age seventeen and the small part I'd played in *All My Sons.*

I've been told that the way I got this role was that Wilder, during a casting conference, said, "Let's not get the same old faces. I'm tired of cliché type-casting—the same people in every film. For the part of Cagney's wife, let's get someone whose face isn't familiar to movie goers—a type like Arlene Francis." (Long, pregnant pause.) "In fact, why don't we get Arlene Francis?"

So far as I am concerned, the only hitch in their getting Arlene Francis was that the picture would be shot in Munich, and that it would necessitate being away from New York for ten weeks. "What's My Line?" was still the mainstay of my television career, and I wasn't sure I could leave it for that length of time. (Horrible thought! What if they got a substitute everybody loved?) Still, I'd never had a vacation or asked for one beyond the four weeks we took every summer, so I approached the Messrs. Goodson-Todman, and they couldn't have been nicer about it. I then made arrangements for a group of substitutes to take over my WOR radio show—Martin would be host now and then, my very good friend Joan Alexander Stanton took it on for a while, and I would record

40

40. Silver Springs (that's Peter in the Brooks Brothers diving gear).
41. My godchild—"She win! She win!"

42. We're speaking Latin, of course.
43. That's Rock Hudson helping to build my ratings on "Luncheon at Sardi's."

THE LEVEL CALL
PURSE $ 15,000
AQUEDUCT N.Y "ARLENE FRANCIS" JULY 21, 1973
PEN-Y-BRYN FARM L. ADAMS up
A. WHITELEY trainer 1 'ls Miles Time 1:
TIR 2nd NORTH OF VENUS 3rd

41

42

43

44. With Jack Klugman in *Tchin-Tchin*. Klugman is on the left.
45. *One, Two, Three*, with James Cagney, in Munich.
46. Portrait by Alvin Gittens

44

45

several shows in advance. When all that was settled, I went out and bought a Berlitz book of useful phrases, brushed up on my schoolgirl German, practicing saying *danke schöen, bitte schöen,* and off I went.

Making the picture was a joy, but even though I found Munich to be a beautiful city, I felt, well, uncomfortable is the word. Here was the scene of the original triumph of bestiality embodied in the person of Adolph Hitler. I knew I ought to be saying, "The war is over, West Germany is our ally, the past is the past," all these things which are patently true, but I simply couldn't help my vestigial bitterness about the war, nor could I forget the horrors the Nazis had inflicted on the world. And though I had promised myself that I wouldn't let it affect my relationship with people with whom I came in contact, I sometimes couldn't help myself. There was this eye doctor, for instance . . .

I had been told that he was a genius in the field of contact lenses, and as I have gone into my sensitivity about my eyes, a doctor would *have* to be a genius to fit me with such lenses. So I consulted the much-touted Herr Doktor, who spoke to me practically not at all. He indicated that I should sit down and where, which I did, and he examined my eyes with a minimum of words, none of which I understood. Berlitz had not prepared me for eye consultations, and for all I know, he might have been saying, "Hey baby, where'dja get them eyes?" but to me the gutturals issuing from him at intervals sounded downright hostile.

He managed to fit me with some lenses that felt like Brillo pads, and wishing to be stoic I merely whimpered, instead of shrieking, as I felt like doing. He paid my tiny pained noises no mind in any case, and when the lenses were in, he said, "Now go avay for ein halb hour, go setzen in der park, go take a valk, und den come back."

He might have *sounded* like Dr. Kronkheit in the old vaudeville sketch, if anyone remembers vaudeville, but he didn't make *me* laugh, I can tell you. I shook my head. "No doctor," I said, "they are already so painful, I cannot wear these lenses for half an hour!"

He fixed me sternly with steely eyes. *"Go sit in der park!"* he ordered, and I said to myself, "If I don't, he'll send me to a concentration camp," and I said, "Yessir, I'll try," and I left.

I walked out of the office in such acute pain that I couldn't stop myself from crying. But with a tremendous exercise of will, I forced myself to stay out for fifteen minutes. Then I went back, and by now the girl behind the reception desk had become, in my mind, Ilse Koch, the Beast of Büchenwald. I pushed past her into the doctor's office and said, "Please take them out right away, this very minute." Without argument, he did, and when they were out I fled from the office and never went back. At this late date, I wish to say that he was probably a very decent, nice man, with a communication problem where I was concerned (and vice versa—after all it was *his* country), but I was in Munich, full of fantasies, and I wasn't taking any chances!

Aside from the Herr Doktor, I had no personal complaint against any of the local citizenry. Whenever we ventured away from the protective aegis of the *One, Two, Three* company, to shop on our own, to go strolling, sightseeing, dining, all of us met with courtesy and kindness, but I could not feel entirely at ease. When Peter's vacation began, he and Martin came over to join me, and Martin felt what I had been feeling with even greater intensity. Peter hadn't even been born during the holocaust, so his interest was purely academic—as one might feel horror reading about the Black Hole of Calcutta, for example, in an abstract way. Our, Martin's and my, feelings were not in the least objective.

It was terribly difficult to connect a city as magnificent as Munich, a city of wide boulevards, beautiful churches and incredible museums, with all the ugliness that had begun in a local beer-hall. I was never able to be totally detached, even though we had as a guide a charming and knowledgeable gentleman. How that happened was that our hotel phone rang one day, I picked it up, and an elegant voice with a combination of German and Oxford accents announced its owner in this way: "Here speaks Francis of Bavaria!"

"Ja ja," I replied, certain that it was one of the *One, Two, Three* comedians, "und here answers Francis of New York."

"I beg your pardon?" came the voice, and I began to blush and stutter, for it came over me that the call might be in earnest. He repeated, "Here speaks Francis of Bavaria, and I am calling at the request of Mr. Drew Dudley of New York."

That settled it. It was a bona fide call, all right, because Drew Dudley is a friend with very impressive, not to say regal, connections all over the world. I've never been in a foreign country that some VIP didn't show up at Drew's behest, to make life easier for me. (Drew's profession is public relations, but these little kindnesses that he does for friends are on a non-professional basis. He just loves bringing people together, which is why he is so good at his job, I suppose.) At any rate, the mention of Drew's name brought forth from me an embarrassed "Eine moment bitte," and I handed the phone over to Martin, who handled things admirably by not even attempting to explain anything, but merely saying "Yes? This is Martin Gabel speaking." He listened for a moment, then said, "Ah of course," in his beautiful, civilized speech. "How very kind of you to call. Mrs. Gabel and I would be delighted, thank you very much indeed. I shall tell her when she returns." (From under the bed, to where she had retired.)

And so it was that Francis of Bavaria became our guide. The nasty word "fascist" never entered the conversation as he took us through the incredible Nymphenburg Museum and all the other glorious places there are to see and enjoy in Munich, and then he brought us back to his charming house for coffee. Class will tell! I knew he really *was* a true prince of the blood, because he never mentioned that insane woman who answered the phone.

A word here about Jimmy Cagney. This, he had decided, would be his last picture. *One, Two Three,* skiddoo. He was a rich man with a jolly, lovable wife, ready to relax and enjoy the sunset years. But on his last picture, he was certainly not going to relax! He was concentrated, dedicated and indefatigable.

Jimmy Cagney himself was a lovely man, a pro, a dedicated, tireless worker. He was also a physical fitness freak! You can learn to hate a man very quickly who spends his lunch hour up in a studio eating yogurt and practicing tap-dancing while you are stuffing yourself with *saüerbraten* and *apfel küchen mit schlag*. I went up and watched him a few times (tappety tap tap side *jump*, side *jump*) and I felt so ashamed of myself that I immediately went on a diet. Jimmy was no youngster at the time, but he certainly looked it, and he was as lithe and nimble as my son Peter.

I think if we'd been shooting the picture in any other country, I'd have had the urge to sightsee in other cities and to visit the rural places and beauty spots (with which I know Germany abounds). I couldn't bring myself to that point, however, and the only time the company left Munich was to go to Berlin, for a scene in the picture which called for Horst Buchholz to ride through East Berlin on a motorcycle, releasing balloons with anti-Russian slogans on them. They weren't supposed to be inflated until he got past the Brandenburg Gate, but by some mischance, one of the armed guards on the roof of one of the buildings caught sight of them and filming was ordered to cease on the spot. The company was invited to leave Berlin forthwith—which you can bet your lederhosen we did. (Back in Munich, our brilliant designer Alex Trammer built us a Brandenburg Gate you couldn't tell from the original.)

New York, though not the miracle of neatness and order that Munich was, looked very good to me, and what with having just played a featured role in an "A" picture, my ego was somewhat restored from the decline it had gone into before I left, and it was reassuring to have "What's My Line?" to come back to.

It was still going strong, and although it *had* yielded a few rating points, it seemed to be holding its own. But no new, sensational offer was awaiting my return. I began to take a rather morbid interest in my mirror, and to dwell on the thought that I might have been a "new face" to Billy Wilder, but so far as television producers and directors were concerned, I'd been so overemployed that I'd become an "old face" long before I was psychologically or chronologically ready for it.

There's such a thing as going too far with this "work ethic" thing. You can get yourself to the point of thinking that if you don't drag yourself into bed at night at the point of exhaustion, you must have been goofing off.

I've got *some* of that in my make-up, but to be honest, that's not all that keeps me—and other performers—flying at breakneck speed whenever possible. It's the inside feeling that if we don't get ourselves into the limelight as often as we can, the public won't see us, and if they don't see us, they forget us. For an actress, a working actress, that's the same as dying.

But with all of that compulsion to stay on the merry-go-round, I hardly know a single professional—and I've had this discussion with dozens and dozens of colleagues—who hasn't said at the height of being busy, "Oh for a quiet time to myself! Oh for a time when I don't have to guard every last word I say in public, when I can have a fight with my husband (or wife) if I feel like it . . . a time to have a broken heart or an operation . . . a time for carelessness . . . !" I've said it myself, one way or another, and maybe I even thought I meant it when I said it.

Well, when I seemed to have come to that point, when there seemed to be a lull in my hectic work schedule, did I do any of those things we'd talked about? Silly question. Of course not! This lifetime habit of momentum didn't get turned off that easily, and I involved myself in everything I was asked to do—went into theater productions all around the country, addressed ladies' clubs, accepted keys to this or that city, and in this whirlwind of make-busy activity, I hoped everyone would see for themselves that I was still younger than springtime and twice as reliable.

(It was just around that time that I was "roasted" at a dinner given in my honor by the Circus Saints & Sinners. It was done with warmth, humor and affection, and of course I was flattered to be the recipient of this honor in this all-male enclave. The "Roast" itself was attended by wives and friends of the members, but it was a men-only club.

For the benefit of some who may not know how these dinners go [in spite of Dean Martin's TV show where they do the same thing], the idea is that the one being honored sits there while various speakers deflate the honoree with—I can't think of another way to describe them—loving insults. Among the speeches at my Roast was one by the "Roastmaster," as he was called, Ted O'Rourke by name, who said, "I asked Martin Gabel when was Arlene's birthday, and he said he didn't know. I said, 'Whaddayamean you don't know? I'm not asking her age, just when is her birthday? Hell, you've been married for sixteen years, so by now you ought to know when her birthday is!' and Martin said, 'How would I know? In sixteen years she's never *had* a birthday!' " I laughed along with everyone else, but in my tenderly sensitive frame of mind, my heart wasn't in it!)

It was also during this have-smile-will-travel period that I was asked to judge the entries in Monaco's annual "Festival du Television" as the United States representative, in company with representatives from other countries.

I had covered the wedding of Princess Grace and Prince Rainier for the *Journal American,* a defunct New York newspaper, and for my "Home" program. It would be a lovely opportunity to pay another visit to that fairy-tale corner of the world, and this time Martin was invited as well. Who could resist? We lunched at the Palace, lost at the Casino and lived in the beautiful Hotel de Paris. I was the only woman among the eleven delegates from various countries, and they gallantly (or spitefully, depending on how you view it!) elected me as president. I remember Marcel Achard, the great French playwright who was also a delegate, twinkling at me, "And what will you do, Miss Francis, when you are locked into a room with all the delegates and they say to you 'What's Your Line?'"

Even the Soviet Union sent a delegate, and as he spoke no English, he had with him an interpreter who spoke both French and English and, it was rumored, was actually a KGB man, sent along to see that the delegate didn't defect with some bikini-clad Monacan.

I have a suggestion for mothers who want to break their children of television viewing. Send them to a TV festival and force them to sit through the whole thing. I don't mean to sound ungrateful to a medium which did so well by me for so long a time, *but*—nine-thirty to five every day?? Think of it—me and my men closeted with ten television sets, all blasting away in tongues which were foreign to *somebody* in the room; reading the Japanese translation, then the Russian, then the Italian, then the French, then the Outer Mongolian. (Yes, I *did* throw that last one in to make it sound hard, but in actual fact I got so dizzy looking and listening that I had to read the *American* translation.) And with everyone puffing away on his native cigarette, even I, an unreconstructed smoker, had teary eyes and could hardly breathe.

At the end of the second or third day, Princess Grace and Prince Rainier were giving us a big dinner party, and much as I love parties and fond as I was of the hosts, I had such a migraine headache from the strain of watching and listening that I couldn't pull myself together sufficiently to make it.

That night, as I lay in bed with compresses on my head,

an adorable Russian doll was delivered to my door, with a note from the representative of the Soviet Union, written in French, telling me how sorry he was that I couldn't attend the dinner and hoping I would feel better and *bien amicalement* and all that, signed Comrade Popov.

The next evening I'd recovered sufficiently to go out, and I got into the same elevator in the hotel with the Russian delegate, his translator, and two other gentlemen. Again I did that dumb thing of speaking loudly and clearly as though that would make him understand me, and I said, "Thank . . . you . . . very . . . much . . . for . . . the . . . *doll!*" rocking my arms back and forth as though I were holding a baby. Tovarich P. looked around furtively to see if the others were watching, but they were engaged in conversation with each other, and so he leaned over to me and in a husky whisper said, "I vood like to keess you!" Sly boots! He'd understood everything everyone had said all along—and no *wonder* they'd sent a watchdog along with him! But I thought later I might have struck a blow for détente if I'd slipped him a little keess!

17

In that list of things I mentioned as wishing I'd had time for was the item "time to fight with your husband." Well, I'm sorry if it sounds boring, but Martin and I have not had the kinds of fights which make their way into gossip columns. Just run-of-the-mill married-people differences which might get serious enough so that I wouldn't speak to him for a day, or vice versa, but neither of us ever packed our bags and made dramatic exits. Perhaps that is because in the really important areas, we generally see eye-to-eye, or if we don't, at least mouth-to-mouth.

The big exception—the instance in which we did *not* see eye-to-eye even after marathon discussions—had to do with Peter's choice of career. Not, of course, that *we* could ultimately decide what he must do with his life. But we could, while he was still trying to make up his mind, guide and influence him—or at least let him know what *we* felt.

Martin is a history buff. His favorite reading (with the possible exception of the *Racing Form*), is in that field of knowledge, and his admiration for the men whose words have rung down through the ages, who have been the movers and shakers of the civilization in which we live, knows no bounds. Where Martin is concerned, however, to be a scholar is not enough. One must be an *articulate* scholar, capable of exerting influence through the power of words.

Peter had done extremely well in school (and honestly, that's not simply Mom-talk—he *did* get elected to Phi Beta Kappa!). Naturally we were filled with pride when we went up to Harvard and saw him graduated *Cum Laude,* and it had already been determined that he would continue at Harvard, in the Law School. Martin had greatly influenced Peter's decision to go to law school, and as Harvard is certainly one of our most prestigious schools, I believe he saw it as a steppingstone to a distinguished career for his son—perhaps even, who knows? a Supreme Court appointment at some future date! It's legitimate to have exalted dreams for one's offspring, even if the offspring doesn't share them—and my suspicion was that that was the case. It was only a suspicion, however, and I said nothing. "Make your mark early," Martin told Peter, "before you are thirty." Harvard Law was, to Martin, the beginning of Peter's making his mark.

The basic problem was that Peter did not feel a strong commitment to the law. It didn't show in his grades, goodness knows—on the contrary! So conscientious is he by nature, that he feels he has an obligation to excel, and in addition he felt it would please his parents—and of course he also felt that even if the law was not his ultimate goal, whatever he did do with his life would not be damaged by having a degree in law.

When eventually we discovered that, my problem was with Martin. I was on Peter's "side" if you can call i. that, in that I felt it *was* his life and that he needed to be happy about what he did with it. I suppose Martin felt abandoned because I couldn't in good conscience join him in his arguments. I thought Peter had earned the right to make his own choice.

How we came to discover how Peter felt was a touch ironic. It was when he was elected to the *Law Review,* a signal honor which quite naturally delighted us. Until, that is, Peter wrote to tell us that he was turning it down. To me, that letter—even though it saddened my husband—ranks with, well, to put it modestly, the Magna Carta or the Declaration of Independence. (You see? You don't have to be Jewish to be a Jewish mother.)

What it said in effect was that he saw the *Law Review* as a commitment to a power drive which he did not have, that it would "limit my opportunities in a rather ironic and insidious way" by inexorably committing him to a certain path of life. He was saying that power and fame were not his bag.

I think that the reason I identified so strongly with Peter was because his letter was in *its* way the same letter I had sent to *my* parents when I felt I had to do something they would be unhappy about—divorce Neil. Both Peter's and my letters were first steps in the direction of maturity, the realization that we must mold our own futures and that we will never be the masters of our souls if we live only to please those we love. Imagine how his closing words dissolved me: "Part of the struggle in all this for me was the simple fact that I love you both very much, and have a great deal of difficulty ever making a decision you disapprove of. . . . " That was exactly how I had felt way back there, and it had taken me a hospital and painful period of psychoanalysis to be able to say it.

(Incidentally, Peter held out a small ray of hope to Martin that all was not yet lost. He included in his letter a probably apocryphal story. The great jurist, Learned Hand, had turned down the *Law Review* the story went, because he wanted free time to play baseball!)

Although Peter took his degree as Doctor of Jurisprudence, Martin eventually came to terms with the fact that he was not going to try for the kind of laurel wreath Martin had envisaged. His initial disappointment has been displaced by a sense of towering pride in having had a hand in rearing a son who is very much his own man—a man who listens with attentive, reasoning courtesy to all suggestions made to him, but makes his own decisions after he has sifted all the information.

(There are times when I wish he was just a shade more manipulable. As one summer, not very long ago, when he showed up in Mount Kisco for a vacation, and we had some discussion on the subject that was national topic A between parents and sons that year—the length of his hair. The most notable aspect of that conversation was that a son of *mine* would turn down the five hundred dollars—*five hundred dollars!*—that I offered him to get a haircut. All right. We both knew it wasn't a serious offer, but if he had said, "I'll take you up on that!" I would have come through. He wouldn't do a thing like that on principle, I imagine, but I wish at that moment he'd had a little less principle and a bit more greed.)

And what *is* our son the lawyer doing now? He is a professor of law and working at getting a doctorate in clinical psychology at the same time. He may not be quite so flamboyant as his parents but his passion for work is positively spectacular. That I understand quite well, since I share it to a degree. Martin is more relaxed in these matters. He believes in working very hard at meaningful things, but he claims there is no point in a frantic compulsion to do whatever is offered just for the sake of being busy. He says that sort of activity impairs one's judgment. Probably true.

On the subject of my devotion to work (by the way, is this getting boring?), magazine interviewers have sometimes treated it as though it were some kind of an oddity, an eccentric quirk in a person who seems on most other counts to be quite rational. *TV Guide,* for example, ran a two-piece article about me entitled "The Amazing Armenian," which devoted a lot of space to the fact that I hate being idle. It illustrated its point with a small anecdote about how, when Billy Wilder called me from California to offer me the role in *One, Two, Three,* I held the receiver in one hand, juggled schedules with the other, and wished I had a third hand so that I could start packing. Then they went on to discuss my alleged earnings, and commented that I had reached a point where I could afford to live exactly as I pleased, and according to them, I was *still* not satisfied.

I didn't want to call it to their attention at the time, but they were missing the point. I *was* living exactly as I pleased. I feel terribly sorry for the people who work *only* so that they will pile up enough money to be able *not* to work. If they've hated what they were doing, what an agony it must have been for them to have to continue doing it day after day.

I don't deny that material benefits are important. It goes without saying that they make life easier and I suppose they represent tangibly a symbol of acceptance in a chosen field. But way beyond that, "exactly as I please" means working as much as possible because I love what I do! "The irony is," the story said, "that she has not yet realized how successful she is," and it flatteringly referred to me as America's third most famous woman. I've got to admit that the poll was taken twenty years ago, and I don't care to have anyone call my attention to more recent polls, if they don't mind. I know a sinking ship when I see one!

The other thing about the story that amused me was the title, "Amazing Armenian." That Armenian background apparently intrigues feature writers. I think it conjures up visions of rug merchants and exotic middle-eastern potentates or something, because it is mentioned so frequently. Or maybe it's that there aren't too many of us around, because a story about me is very apt to include the names of William Saroyan, Rouben Mamoulian, Michael Arlen and an assortment of other gifted people whose names either end in "-ian" or a facsimile, or have been changed from something that did. I don't *mind* being lumped with them, in fact I enjoy being in such exalted company, but it *does* strike me as a bit odd. It's as though they were to lump Martin with Elizabeth Taylor, which would be lovely lumping too, because they are both Jewish performers. I don't think Martin would mind that either, but it simply doesn't seem pertinent.

To prove that money isn't always the prod where I am concerned, I was delighted when I was elected a member of the board of directors of Bonwit Teller (or rather of the 721 Corporation, which owned Bonwit's, which was in turn the child of the parent corporation, Genesco, and whoever said big business was uncomplicated?) Board of Directors! (Now *there*, Daddy would have thought, was a phrase with a ring to it!)

When I said yes, that I would be honored to serve on the board, I hadn't a clue what Bonwit Teller had in mind for me. As I told newspaper people at the time, "Perhaps they want to take advantage of all that experience I had on the 'Home' show in dealing with the fashion world. I may be able to suggest things which would be beguiling to women, things to do with color and design—who knows? At any rate, it sounds like an exciting challenge, and of course I'm honored to be the first and *only* woman on a board with seventeen men!"

The seventeen were presidents of insurance companies, corporate heads, bankers—there were wheeler-dealer types in many fields. None of them were there to get rich, that's certain, because we all drew the same stipend—one hundred dollars per meeting, and a maximum of four meetings per year. So much for my money-mad motivation! I also owned a minuscule amount of stock in Genesco, but I wasn't on that board to protect *that*. No, it was the new experience it represented, the look at a totally different facet of American life—the world of business—which fascinated me.

Well sir, I was on that board for eighteen years, until it was dissolved, and the only time I ever spoke up on a subject upon which I would have presumed they would want to hear from me, I got a patient smile and a deaf ear. It was at the time that the fashion industry was trying to commit suicide by pushing long skirts onto women in place of the minis they had come to love so well. I asked to be heard on the subject.

"Gentlemen," I said in my throatiest member-of-the-board voice, "to put it plainly, this is a disaster. There is simply not enough *time* to promote so radical a change. The eye has to get accustomed to a new look, and just because Paris and *Women's Wear Daily* says they have to, it doesn't mean that American women are going to snap to attention and salute. I don't think they're going to buy those clothes."

There was a silence around the table, and the man who was president of Genesco at the time stood up and addressed me. In a condescending "there-there-little-girl" voice he said, "Arlene, in four months when we have our next meeting, I'm going to ask you to stand up and repeat what you have just said!" The board seemed relieved. The economy had been saved.

Now that's the kind of argument one doesn't want to win, and when the "new look" turned out to be a disaster, I was certainly not smug about having been right. Not only Bonwit's, but hundreds of stores across the nation suffered frightful losses, and the fashion industry went into a slump from which many friends in the industry tell me it has only recently emerged. As a stockholder I was appalled at what had happened, but as a woman I had a sneaky sense of pride in the fact that we hadn't proved to be that predictable, that we refused to be led like sheep into buying things we didn't like. Women had looked at the greatest art work the advertising departments could devise, at the most beautiful models in the world adorning the fashion pages of magazines, had read the most glittering copy the nimble minds of ad writers could create, and their response had been a loud and decisive "NO!" They simply took their last year's dresses out of the closet and left the stores stocked with millions of dollars worth of merchandise which could hardly be *given* away at sale time.

I count those years on the board as a fascinating learning experience. I wouldn't have dreamed that I could get that absorbed in talk about square feet of space, mark-ups, budgets, billing systems, trends in merchandising and so on, but I did.

■

Another non-paying job came my way—this one as a result of my international fame as a scholar. If you don't accept that version of how I came to sit on the Council of the University of Utah, try this one: I'd gone out to Salt Lake City to play in the university's theater, in a production of *Old Acquaintance*, a play by John Van Druten that had starred Jane Cowl and had been a big hit way back when. A close friend, Mary Cooper, and I were the only professionals in the company. The rest were students, and I agreed to play in it because I believe whole-heartedly in regional theater. It's one of the few places left for performers in this country to discover how they might fit into the theater world and get the training they need at the same time.

I've seen some of the most remarkable productions done in remote places—imaginative, original, talented—and I'm always rocked backwards when I see things like that because I'm just insular enough so that when anyone says "Theater," my automatic reflex says "New York." But here I was, a thousand miles from Broadway, in a magnificently equipped theater, with a company of people whose professionalism left nothing to be desired.

As it happened, the public relations woman for the university, Bets Haglund, had been our public relations woman on NBC's "Home," and she called to ask if I would enjoy sitting in on a few classes, and would I examine their dance program, to all of which I said yes, of course I would.

When I did, I kept shaking my head in wonder. *Way out here,* I repeated to myself, *imagine all this going on way out here.* Parochial thinking? Yes, of course; exactly in line with that wonderfully comic map of the United States which was once on the cover of the *New Yorker* magazine. Most of the map was occupied by New York City, and here and there were dots labelled Dubuque (dyed-in-wool New Yorkers' name for most places which aren't New York) and then there was an area called West Coast—and that was it. I know that people around the country resent New Yorkers for this attitude about their own Big Apple, but they really shouldn't, because after all, New York City belongs to everyone. If a great deal of the action centers there, it is action which has been generated by people from all over the country—the world, for that matter.

At any rate, clearly the University of Utah had a stunning, comprehensive theatrical training program, and when it was suggested that the program would benefit enormously by having somebody actually involved professionally in the arts who would sit on the council board, and that they would like that somebody to be me, I enthusiastically agreed to do it.

As with the Bonwit Teller board, I was the outsider, so to speak. What I didn't have on *this* board that the others did have, was a string of letters after my name—you can't count a couple of doctorates in the humanities as scholastic achievement. I discovered, however, that it was neither scholarship nor advice on stagecraft that my learned colleagues wanted from me. It was my ability as a saleswoman! As with most institutions that are dependent on the generous donations of interested people for their continued existence, the first business of the council was business. They had to raise money to keep their lively program going, for without funds, there are no little gem-like theaters, no arts programs—for that matter there are no history, literature, math or science programs either. Man may not live by bread alone, but it takes many loaves of bread to get the rest of the things man likes to live by.

I agreed to talk to alumni and other interested groups in my "neighborhood"—the New York area, that is—because obviously I couldn't go around the country beating the drums unless I wanted people to start making donations to *me*. After doing this for a while, it became clear to me that I couldn't do an effective job for the university on so haphazard a basis, so very reluctantly I withdrew from the council.

I have a portrait which is a wonderful reminder to me of that period. It was painted by the university's artist-in-residence, Alvin Gittens, and was presented to me in a ceremony where all we scholars embraced each other and the band played the alma mater. It hangs in my library to remind my friends that no matter what *they* think, I am no stranger to the Halls of Academe!

For scoffers, I have other credentials—I am an Overseer of Emerson College in Boston, and yes, I will admit there is an element of hometown-girl-makes-good there, but largely I continue to function as an overseer because I consider Emerson to be a superb school in the field of communications, and I feel myself to be part of that field. I do as much as I can for them—enough to justify my staying on, because it is a cardinal principle with me never to go on any board or allow my name to be used on a letterhead of any organization in which I do not actively participate. I don't like policies to be made in my name if I have nothing to do with initiating them.

About those doctor of humanities degrees I mentioned—I picked up one from American International College at Springfield, Massachusetts, and one from Keuka College in New York State. When I was awarded the second of those degrees, they started calling me Double Doctor around the house, but I still don't know how to spell and my knowledge of syntax is negligible. There's higher education for you.

18

"END OF THE LINE" was the heading on one of the stories dealing with the fact that "What's My Line?" was going off the air after seventeen-and-a-half years. As dependable as death and taxes and a good bit more amusing than either—the show had succumbed to the public's inexorable appetite for change. The public itself had changed, in fact—the generation of "Mouseketeer" watchers had grown up.

By show business standards, "What's My Line?" was an antiquity. Except for "The Ed Sullivan Show," nothing had run so long or been so consistently entertaining, but the ratings had slipped and CBS had shaken its corporate head and said, "Sorry, gang." We still had millions of viewers, but the surveys showed that they were mostly over forty, and there was a new kid in town whom everyone wanted to get on the good side of named Youth.

The implications (at least to me) were pretty frightening. If the *show* was an antique, what about the panelists? Was I going to have to sit back with nothing to do but watch my arteries harden from there on in? I remember the last show, when John Daly took the Mystery Guest spot, answering all our questions in a childish falsetto. I guessed him rather quickly and said, "Is this the new Voice of America, John?" Were all fashion, all entertainment, all manners and mores to be the exclusive province of the under-thirty group from there on in?

It certainly would have seemed so, and indeed, *was* there ever another time in our or anyone else's history that a particular *age* group took over as did the youth of the 60s? I don't mean simply the normal processes whereby youth replaces age on a gradual basis—if that did not happen, how else could the world survive? No, I am speaking of the fact that the 60s produced a phenomenon, a surging tidal wave which threatened to engulf everyone who had recovered from acne.

I would have had to be blind and deaf not to be aware of the dramatic changes which were apparent on all fronts. They had been apparent for a long time before "What's My Line?" went off the air, but I submit that even in the middle of social revolutions, people seldom stop and say, "Wow! Am I living in turbulent times!" Unless you happen to be one of the planners of the turbulence or an active participant, the chances are very much that you go along trying to make a living, adjusting to changes in your society as best you can, deploring or approving perhaps, but on the whole just trying to get along.

In my own area, entertainment, I was more aware of a diminishing of standards (or so I viewed it) than of sweeping changes. Things were beginning to creep into the theater for which I had very little taste, but in the beginning, I didn't see them as crowding out what I *do* go to the theater to see. I merely shrugged and told myself there was room for everything.

On the theory that I ought to understand what was going on, I even persuaded Martin to take me to see *Oh! Calcutta!* and the result of that little sortie into the sewer was not what one would have predicted. It was Martin who left at the end of the first act, not so much disgusted as bored with what he regarded as a collection of stale, dirty jokes. *I* felt I had an obligation to stay to the bitter end, and when I finally slunk out of the theater (hoping nobody would recognize me, covered as I was in a plain brown wrapper), I kept repeating to myself, "This too shall pass."

Proves again what a great prophet I am. Not only didn't it pass, I understand there have been some shows since then which make *Oh! Calcutta!* look like dramatizations of *A Child's Garden of Verses*. I don't know first-hand because I don't attend them. (I didn't even go to see *Hair*, which I understand had some "redeeming social values" in that it had an anti-Viet Nam war theme. I approved of the theme, but I heard nothing about the show that led me to believe it had any redeeming *theatrical* values, which would seem to me to be the first aim of doing a show. All anyone talked about was that some naked actors stood on the stage at the end of the first act, to which I could only say "big deal." Nobody hummed any lovely tunes to me, or quoted any bright dialogue, so I stayed home.) (Yes, I'm aware it has earned millions. It doesn't change my mind about what I go to the theater to see.)

While I was still suffering withdrawal pains from being without "What's My Line?" to go to on Sunday nights, I was given an opportunity to lift my spirits with four glorious weeks in London.

I went to the theater, saw the sights, sampled the best London had to offer in the way of restaurants and museums (and that's mighty good sampling), met old friends and made new ones, and walked the streets I loved. But I hadn't gone there for any of those things. I'd gone to work in a TV drama which we were filming there, and *that* part, unfortunately became a disaster area.

It had looked so good on paper. It was an adaptation of a screen classic, *Laura,* rewritten for television by Truman Capote, and I believe the reason he wrote it was to furnish a vehicle in which to introduce his very good friend Lee Radziwill to the world as an actress. The world already had met her as the sister of Jacqueline Bouvier Kennedy Onassis, and for a lady as beautiful and bright as Lee (at that time Princess Radziwill), it was probably not too easy always to have to take second billing to her sister.

Lee is someone I admire. She is intelligent, perceptive and a woman of superb taste, and if these qualities, combined with her beauty, could make an actress of her, she has them in sufficient quantity to make Katharine Cornell look like an amateur in the high school play. One can learn to be a competent performer, one can be directed not to bump into the furniture, or to project, or any number of other things, but to qualify as an *actress* requires something more, and Lee simply had not had the experience to acquire the "something more" at that point.

David Susskind was the producer of this program, and was going all out to assure a first-class production. It was a fantastically costly venture, and it rested largely on the slim shoulders of Lee Radziwill. To bring it off, she would have had to have the same capacity to captivate an audience that

Gene Tierney had had in the original film, and I believe she was all too aware of that.

To add to that heavy pressure, she was moving in fast company—professionals of the calibre of George Sanders, Robert Stack, Farley Granger and even me, so it couldn't have been very easy for her. She is much too sensitive a person not to have known that she'd get a lot of flak from the press if she didn't do well, on the who-does-she-think-she-is order. There was bound to be resentment against an amateur who had gotten a role because of who she was rather than what she could do. And goodness knows, that was true—but I think she would have argued that it would be equally unfair to *deprive* her of a role because of who she was, and that after all, the only reason Truman had agreed to write it was because *she* was doing it. And that was true too. One thing nobody could fault her on was her determination, and as I wrote to Martin at the time, "She's very attractive and gentle on the outside, but like Jackie, I think she has a very solid underpinning."

Our caretaker in London, before Susskind arrived, was Alan Shayne (now a V.I.P. at Warner's) and a more gentle shepherd does not exist. He did his best to make us happy, but every theatrical company develops its own aura, good or bad, and the aura around *Laura* was not something to adora. There was a rather bristling quality about it, hostilities cropping up here and there, and a general feeling of uneasiness. There was also one continuous feud between two of the actors which made everyone very nervous. It erupted one day in a name-calling contest, with one of the combatants saying, "You're obnoxious in this part!" and the other replying, "Yes, I hope so because I've rehearsed being obnoxious, but you seem to have achieved it quite naturally." It was petty and spiteful, and I think none of it would have happened if we hadn't all felt a sense of doom about the project.

Aside from the personality problems, nobody was satisfied with Truman's script, so it was constantly being rewritten. There were times when I was sure the whole thing was going to be called off, and perhaps it would have been better if it had, for when it was finally shown, it proved to be one of television's spectacular failures.

En passant, I would like to add a kind word for David Susskind, who didn't get too many of those as the result of his efforts. He was encouraging and he tried. When he came from America he made every effort to bolster our spirits and not to show his own disappointment at what he must have known, along with the rest of us who knew about such things—that he was sitting in on a terminal case.

Aside from *Laura*, London that year was a revelation. I'd been there so often in the past, I regarded it as another home—thought I knew it inside out—but this was a London I'd never seen before. This was the "Swingin' London" I'd seen proclaimed in the travel ads, and everything I had begun to feel about changes in the United States was amplified about a thousand per cent here. It was a shocker to me, for I had always thought of England as the *sanctum sanctorum* in matters of taste and of graceful elegance.

As I walked the streets in dazed surprise, I remembered what a friend of mine had said, that everyone looked as though they were headed for a Hallowe'en party. They were wearing costumes, and the terrible thought struck me that if everyone did *that,* why would anyone have to go to the theater? I knew that the men were letting their hair grow in the States, but even so I had a sense of shock when the beauty who was tinting my hair turned out to be a boy—his own locks almost waist length. (A cockney boy at that, who said things such as "I fink the color's gowing to tyke!")

And just as at home, there were no signs up which said "WATCH YOUR STEP! SOCIAL REVOLUTION IN PROGRESS!" Nevertheless, you had only to take a walk along the King's Road of a Saturday afternoon to know that there'd been some changes made. The freak parade had certainly replaced the Tower of London and Canterbury Cathedral as the number-one tourist attractions. The costumed, spangled, booted, bearded, weirdo, zonked-out youth brigade, the funky little stores, the blasting rock heard everywhere—believe me, compared to King's Road, Greenwich Village was still quaint and quiet. Or perhaps that was because I was looking at it with the eyes of a tourist, something I'd never had time to do in New York—but no, I really think London was a few years in advance of us in ringing in the era of alienation from everything that had gone before.

I didn't care much for any of it, although I wrote to Martin rather light-heartedly that even some people *I* knew in the theater world—not just the kids—had adopted the degenerate pirate look, complete with scraggly long hair and untidy whiskers. I found it rather unattractive, but I clung to the notion that it was all temporary insanity and that sooner or later everyone would go back to bathing.

Besides, an awful lot of people still wore their bespoke suits and expensive cravats, lived in elegant digs which were candle-lighted, fireplaced, flower-bowered and wooden-paneled, and they set their tables with crystal, silver and linen. But, no question about it, the mood was clearly mod, and it was spreading outward from King's Road and Carnaby Street into Mayfair. And as in the United States, the changes were not merely sartorial.

To stay with the area I know best, the theater, the changes were very disconcerting in my view. An import, *America Hurrah!* was packing them in, a hit with not only the young to whom it addressed itself, but with elderly critics who I rather suspected were afraid of being thought old-hat if they happened not to like it. More and more there were offerings in theaters for which I had no appetite—things which seemed to me to be strident, tuneless, in a curious way anti-intellectual, deliberately ugly, and hiding a prurient appeal behind an alleged social message.

But badly shaken as I was by all these new manifestations, I was cheered by the fact that *olde* England was still very much in evidence, side by side with swingin' London, and merry as it had always been.

At the opposite pole from King's Road was Ascot, for example, where you wouldn't know there'd ever been such a thing as a youth revolution. I went there one day when there was a benefit to raise funds for cancer research, and in keeping with my policy of improving each shining hour, I took my tape recorder along so that I could interview some of the denizens of the track for the benefit of my WOR audience.

I went there with a friend of ours named Lady D'Avigdor Goldsmid, which sounds very imposing indeed, so we call her Rosie, which suits her rollicking informality much better. Lady Goldsmid came into our lives via a good friend in New York, who said, "When you get to London, call Rosie. You'll adore each other. She's just the best lady in England."

I took her literally, thinking she meant a small "l" lady, so when I called the number I'd been given, I asked for Mrs.

Goldsmid. A rather haughty upstairs-downstairs maid said, "There's naow Mrs. Goldsmid heah."

I said, "Do I have MAY 0505?"

"Yiss meddim, thees ees MAY 0505, but theah ees naow Mrs. Goldsmid heah."

"That's odd," I said, "Mrs. Backer gave me this number."

Her holiness replied, "Aow, we knaow Mrs. Backah."

"Eef yew knaow Mrs. Backah," I said, "then theah must be a Mrs. Goldsmid."

"Aow," she aowed, "*Lady* Goldsmid is in the Saouth of Frawnce. Dew yew want her numbeh?"

"No," I replied, "Just tell her Princess Arlene called." I may say I've been that ever since to darling Rosie Goldsmid.

Rosie knew everyone at Ascot and made sure that I met them all—Loelia the Duchess of Westminster, and someone who sounded like the Maharanee of Double Whammy, and like that. (I interviewed the former, and the latter put me on to a good nag which sent me home a big winner.) Rosie also trotted out a parade of brisk young people who seemed all to be named Pam and Cynthia and Colin and Ian, and a goodly group of bowlered blokes and genteel powdered ladies, reasonably ancient but not nearly so ancient as their clothes—bits of fur that would embarrass a mouse, raincoats to the ankles, cloche hats at half tilt and jackets at half mast. It wouldn't have surprised me in the least to see Eliza Doolittle in the crowd yelling *"Move your bloody arse!"* to the horses, it was all so *My Fair Lady*-ish.

And in between King's Road at one end and Ascot at the other, there was a lot going on that I *could* understand, including some marvelous theater. I remember seeing a performance of *As You Like It* which had me reeling with admiration, for I must confess that although we have some excellent Shakespearean actors in our own country (including my husband!), one gets the feeling that English actors must be weaned on Shakespeare, so immense is their understanding and communication. There was, in fact, plenty of theater for me to see in London, including a superb performance by my dear friend Constance Cummings, with Sir Laurence Olivier in O'Neill's *Long Day's Journey into Night*.

Yes, the old England was very much in evidence still—in country weekends at Rosie's, where the serene English countryside put my soul at rest, as it always does. And there were cozy evenings with American friends who lived in London, such as the Charles Collingwoods and the John Crosbys, and with Constance Cummings and her fine English playwright husband, Benn Levy. A special joy was the reunion with Peter Viertel—a friend since my early Hollywood days, and his ravishing wife, Deborah Kerr. At the homes of all these people, I met new English friends who shaved and took baths and talked about Lytton Strachey and Rupert Brooke and made me wish Martin were there to raise the perceived level of American scholarliness, and which also made me forget for a moment that Out There, they were crowding my generation.

One of the changes in London which won my heartiest approval was the new wave of excellent restaurants, for whatever other virtues it had had, London had never been known as a gourmet's paradise. Now however, lovely, fattening places were springing up everywhere, and I have saved out a menu from a madly popular place called Nick's Diner. It offered "Steak, kidney, mushroom and oyster pie, 15/6, a dear old favourite which is belly-comforting rather than adventurous," and "Tomatoes guacamole, 6/, fresh tomatoes which have their insides scooped out and are stuffed with a peppery avocado puree, a process which sounds much crueller than it is."

As long as that sort of thing went on, I felt England was still merry. In fact, as long as there is an England, it couldn't be any other way. I could forget the revolution. The only bomb visible was *Laura*.

A few months after returning to America, I heard to my joy that "What's My Line?" had been given a reprieve. It was coming back on the screen in a new format, mostly a daytime but sometimes a nighttime show, five times a week, syndicated around the country.

I had very mixed feelings about it, to tell the truth—delighted of course to be back on television on a regular basis, but dismayed that I was the only one of the original panel to be on the show. As it was to be directed toward a different age group, how would *I* fare? I wasn't ready to be the grey eminence, and I didn't want my fellow panelists calling me "Big Mama."

Our moderator was a very able young man named Wally Bruner, and on the first show, the other panelists were the wild Soupy Sales, Joanna Barnes and the remarkable actor

Alan Alda. Joanna's and Alan's were swing positions, changed frequently, but Soupy was steady. I was relieved that nobody helped me into my chair or treated me with respect on that first show.

At first I desperately missed the "good old days" and my former colleagues. Everything was different, it seemed to me, including the type of guests we had. Gone, in my opinion, was the good taste of yesteryear. In its place were the anything-goes occupations; strippers, *Guinness Book of Records'* longest kisser, a hen that could play "Yankee Doodle" on the piano with her beak—what did it matter? If it got a laugh, it was okay.

I found myself nursing stabs of resentment which I kept under wraps, but do you know something? It came over me one day that I was getting a bit yesteryear myself, and that if I didn't watch it, I'd be in a powdered wig and carrying a walking stick, shaking it at young whippersnappers. It was agonizing reappraisal time, moment-of-truth we call it in the theater, and I came to a decision—get with it or get out of it. I would relax and try to enjoy what *was* happening, rather than brood about what used to happen.

Up until that moment, I had secretly thought of Soupy as a bona fide nut. With the hostility gone, I was able to see him for what he was, a very shrewd, very able young comedian with a superb sense of timing, who was unquestionably attracting an entirely new audience. Our M.C., Wally Bruner, may not have been John Daly, but why did he have to be? As Wally Bruner he had plenty to recommend him, and indeed he was so good that he left us because I think they gave him the state of Indiana. He was replaced by Larry Blyden (whose shining career came to a tragic end with a fatal accident in Africa, where he was vacationing)—again different, but by then I'd learned that *different* doesn't have to be a pejorative word.

All those "different" people and "different" occupations I'd had such reservations about pleased enough of an audience to keep "What's My Line?" going for another eight years, something which obviously the Old Guard hadn't been able to do. For all I know it still shows up on screens here and there, and this experience taught me a valuable lesson: that *new*, while it is not necessarily good, is also not necessarily bad!

19

The longer you sit on top of a mountain, the harder it is to come down. Something happens to your heart and lungs in all that rarified air, which makes it difficult to breathe if you're suddenly catapulted down to street level.

About a year before "What's My Line? went off the air, the thought struck me that I'd been up there way on top for an uncommonly long time, filling my lungs with the sweet air of success, enjoying the scenery to the fullest, and maybe I'd better start thinking about climbing down. Not precipitously, not a plunge—but carefully, one step at a time.

There'd been straws in the wind, hints here and there that I might no longer be the biggest thing since sliced bread. One such was when Barbara Walters changed networks, and while nothing had changed my mind about "Today" and I'd never regretted not doing it, I *did* think about Barbara's other show on that network, "Not for Women Only," as something that would be right for me. Accordingly, I dropped a note to a vice president, who was a friend of mine, in which I said that I hoped that while they were considering people to take the show over, they would throw my name into the hopper as a possibility.

I had a call as soon as he received it, and was advised they had already made a decision before he got my note. It just hadn't occurred to them, he said, that I would be interested! The point, of course, is that just a few years back I probably would have been the first person he would have thought of. As I say, I'm glad that I had already started to make my psychological preparations for this sort of thing, for otherwise it would have sent me into a depression.

One learns along the way not to confuse "movement" with action. Movement can be fruitless, whereas action has aim. Where I no longer have the wide choice of jobs which I once had, I am thoroughly happy with my daily WOR radio program. It entertains and educates me, and in all modesty I believe it does the same for my audience. My changed status in no way influences me to do things that I would consider to be onerous chores, or which would offend my own particular standards of taste.

I am aware that there is a faintly Victorian overtone when one speaks of "standards of taste" in an era when anything goes. The revolution which I first noted in London a decade ago and which I thought of as a passing fancy fooled me by becoming entrenched. As it affected the theater, the social message has long since gone by the boards, but the prurience lingers on, and though I've gotten used to it, I haven't gotten to like it any better.

I still cannot accept stag party talk as an adequate substitute for dialogue, unless, of course, it's a scene involving a stag party. And what I positively cannot forgive is that the casual use of such talk has wrought mayhem on the beautiful English language, has done it damage from which it may never recover. I don't like the obligatory fornication scene in movies, dragged in by the, excuse the expression, tail, as a rule, because I'm convinced that producers are afraid to leave it out. Same thing with the obligatory nude scene on the stage. In fact I went to see a hugely successful play recently in which an actress played an entire scene with bared breasts for no discernible reason. True, she was supposed to be seductive, but I felt she would have been a good deal more so in her clothes, since the audience so concentrated on what they were seeing that they heard nothing of what was being said. It was mentioned in all the reviews and maybe it attracted some customers, but if that was why they came, they'd have been a lot better off in a porn house on 42nd Street.

When you start pursing up your lips about nudity and obscenity and so on, it's bound to give you pause about yourself. "Am I really a prig?" I ask myself, and in fact it worried me so much at one point that I talked it over with Peter, not on a mother-son level, but on a generation-to-generation basis. I explained to him that I have First Amendment trouble every time I pass a newsstand these days, that as a liberal I suffer from the dichotomy that commits me to freedom of the press and a firm stand against censorship on the one hand, but makes me want to sweep all that filth into the gutter on the other hand.

What I actually asked Peter was whether he thought that my having certain "standards of decency" opened me to the charge of being "old-fashioned" or whatnot. I told him how I felt about nudity, about obscenity and so forth, and he wrote me his reply:

. . . Your reaction to nudity has always seemed quite personal to me. You have never objected to a nakedness which is intended to be in some way expressive of a human tenderness; yet you are opposed to obscenity which is anti-human—that is, which has at its heart some cruelty or degradation of desire. I think if the nudity in *Equus* offended "society's standards of decency" then you would oppose those standards and would support the play—while if you were asked your opinion of *Hustler* magazine, it would be negative whether or not Society's standards were for it. That some of my generation are contemptuous of their sexuality does not make you "prudish" for seeing them as they in fact are. (And if anyone says different they can go fuck themselves.)

Of course none of this has anything to do with whether one supports or opposes obscenity laws. If we want *Ulysses* then of course *Hustler* must print what it likes. Repression is always worse than perversity because perversity at least has a voice; it allows suffering to be seen rather than keeping it hidden. . . .

Peter's letter helped me to put into focus some of the things I think and to separate them from what I feel—which isn't always the same thing. It also made me reflect that I have travelled a very long distance, several light years I should think, from a time of *King Arthur's Round Table* to a discussion of Larry Flynt's *Hustler* magazine. The changes along the way have been monumental, but it has been a terrific trip so far, with hardly a dull moment and a million surprises along the way.

I'd like to share one of the most recent of these, because it was something that I think will make a difference in my life.

In the theater, there is something called "the moment of truth," in which a character stands revealed in his true colors, stripped of pretense, of his props for living. In life there are such moments too, and I believe most of us have had those revelations in which we suddenly see ourselves more clearly. That is precisely what happened to me when I was listening to the play-back of an interview I had done with the authors of a book that dealt with the meaning of dreams.

It's a fascinating subject, I think, and in the course of the interview I told my guests about a recurrent dream of my own; I pick up a phone to make a call, and discover it has no mouthpiece. I seek another phone, and it is the same—there is no mouthpiece. In panic, I go from phone booth to phone booth, in and out of rooms, unable to find a telephone with a mouthpiece, frantic in my drive to communicate with someone—anyone.

"But," from the Olympian heights of my Freudian know-how, I told my guests, "I know the meaning of that dream. It's just basic frustrations. I presume it represents my anxiety about my career as an actress."

Later, listening to the play-back, I had that moment of truth I mentioned. Frustration, yes—but the dream had nothing to do with my career. In a flash of understanding, I realized how deeply my inability to express myself without becoming apprehensive about what "they" might think had affected me. In short, my "don't make waves" philosophy had inhibited my life to an incalculable extent, for in my desire to keep things peaceful all the time, I had forgotten that a few waves are necessary to keep the water from becoming stagnant.

It doesn't sound like an earthshattering discovery, I know, but I tell it to point up something that I think *is* important: the learning process is never-ending, and growth will continue if only you will allow it to.

As I see life now, it is constant discovery along a road, and I look eagerly forward to the rest of the journey.

Index

✳ It has come to my attention that in certain circles, there are those people who immediately look at the index of a book to see if their names are included. As luck would have it, I have friends in those circles who happen not to have participated in the events included in these pages. Still, they are a part of my life, and I cannot conceive of a book dealing with me which does not include mention of them—at least in the *index*.

Here, then, is the entire cast—players and non-players alike!

"Betty and Bob," 31, 44
Big Fish, Little Fish, 66
"Big Sister," 26, 31, 52
Billingsley, Sherman, 80
Billy Reed's Little Club, 87, 100
Blackwell, Earl, *199
Blass, Bill, *199
"Blind Date" (radio program), 49–
    51, 71, 72
"Blind Date" (television program),
    85, 88–90
Block, Hal, 93
Blyden, Larry, 194
Bogart, Humphrey, 76
Bowles, Paul, 43
Bradman, Sir Don, 99
Bren, Milton, *199
Bren, Claire. *See* Trevor, Claire
Brinkley, David and Susan, *199
BBC, 98
Bronfman, Edgar, *199
Brooks, Donald, *199
Bruner, Wally, 193–94
Buchholz, Horst, 173
Buchwald, Ann and Art, *199
Burke, Billie, 28
Burrows, Abe, 51, 64, 122
Bushkin, Joey, *199
Butz, Carol ("Bootzie"), 132

Cagney, Jimmy, 169, 172
Cahan, Dr. William and Grace
    (Mirabella), *199
Caldwell, Zoe, *199
Calhern, Lou, 63, 64, 66, 73, 79–
    81, 86, 125
Cannon, Jimmy, 63, 64, 66, 79
Cannon, Poppy, 138, 139
Capote, Truman, 130, 188–89
Carlisle, Kitty, 124, 126
Carter, Amy, 113–14
Carter, Jimmy, 31, 113–14, 156
Carter, Rosalynn, 114, 156
"Cavalcade," 26
Cavett, Dick, 97
Cerebral Palsy Foundation, 145
Cerf, Bennett, 93, 94, 97, 100–101,
    125, 127, 130, 137
Cerf, Jonathan, 118
Cerf, Phyllis, 124, 127, 137
Chodorov, Edward, *199
Chodorov, Jerome, 57, 63, 64
Chodorov, Rhea, 63, 64
Circus Saints & Sinners, 174
Clurman, Harold, *199
Clurman, Richard and Shirley,
    *199
Colbert, Claudette, 32
College Humor, 18
Collingwood, Mr. and Mrs.
    Charles, 193
Colman, Ronald, 77

CBS, 186
Columbia Journal, 18
Comden, Betty, 122, 125
Considine, Bob, 100
Cooper, Mary, 57, 183
Cooper, Wyatt and Gloria
    (Vanderbilt), 130, *199
Cornell, Katharine, 53
Cornell Widow, 18
Corwin, Norman, *199
Cotten, Joseph, 31, 43, 163–64
Coward, Noel, 68
Cowl, Jane, 183
Crane, Muriel, 144
Cronin, John, *199
Cronkite, Walter and Betsy, *199
Cronyn, Hume, and Jessica
    (Tandy), *199
Crosby, Mr. and Mrs. John, 193
Crouse, Russell, 70
Cummings, Constance, 192, 193
Cup of Trembling, 83–84
Curtis, Charlotte, *199
Cusick, Peter and Edla, *199
Custin, Mildred, *199
Czinner, Paul, 83, 85

Daly, John, 90, 94, 98, 99–101, 186
Danton's Death, 32, 42–43
D'Arlene Studios, 20–22
Davis, Albert, 8–11, 20
Davis, Bette, 48, 97
Davis, Glenn, 141
Dead End Kids, 53
Deal, Dr. C. Pinckney, *199
DeWolfe, Ashley, 16–17
Dickerson, Nancy and Dick, *199
Diener, Joan, 51, 64
Dietz, Howard and Lucinda
    (Ballard), *199
Dinner at Eight, 103, 104
Dirksen, Senator Everett, 97
Don, Uncle, 49
Donen, Stanley, 130
Doughgirls, The (Fields), 54, 55–58
Douglas, Kirk, 31
Douglas, Sharman, *199
Dowling girls, 79
Downey, Morton and Anne, *199
Downs, Hugh, 138, 143, 159, 161
Duchin, Peter and Cheray, *199
Dudley, Drew, 157, 171–72

"Ed Sullivan Show, The," 186
Elizabeth II, Queen of England, 31
Ellington, Duke, 31
Emerson, Faye, 31
Equus, 197
Erskine, Chester, 82

Fadiman, Clifton, 51, 64
Fair, Mildred, *199